COPPER Magic!

COPPER Magic!

NO-FAIL RECIPES FOR THE
Revolutionary New Nonstick Cookware

ELLA SANDERS

CASTLE POINT BOOKS
NEW YORK

www.castlepointbooks.com
www.stmartins.com

The Castle Point Books trademark is owned by Castle Point Publications, LLC.
Castle Point books are published and distributed by St. Martin's Press.

ISBN 978-1-250-17359-1 (trade paperback)
ISBN 978-1-250-17360-7 (eBook)

Design by Katie Jennings Campbell
Production by Tara Long
Images provided by Allan Penn or used under license from Shutterstock.com.

Our books may be purchased in bulk for promotional, educational, or
business use. Please contact your local bookseller or the Macmillan Corporate
and Premium Sales Department at 1-800-221-7945, extension 5442,
or by e-mail at MacmillanSpecialMarkets@macmillan.com.

First Edition: September 2017

10 9 8 7 6 5 4 3 2 1

Contents

Introduction

COPPER COOKWARE has always had something of a mystique; an old copper teapot on the stove or a shiny copper sauce pot warming up over the flames can make you feel as though you're cooking in the kitchen of a quaint French chateau. But now, copper pans are making a comeback for different reasons. These beautiful pans are completely nonstick, taking away the frustration of scraping away at caked-on food, remaking ruined recipes, or having to purchase new cookware to replace the old, damaged ones. They're also heat conductive! This means that the pan will heat up evenly every time you cook. You'll never worry again about unevenly cooked food or constantly fiddling with the heat to get your meal prepared just right.

In this book, you'll find more than 75 recipes to make the most of your copper pan. Many of the recipes, such as the Garden-Fresh Frittata, Buttermilk Fried Chicken, or Giant Apple Pie, are perfect when cooked in a deep copper square pan. Others, such as the Flaky Biscuit Pizzas, the Ginger-Kiwi Chicken Quesadillas, or the Egg Scramble on Avocado Toast, don't require the deep pan and are great for a 12-inch copper pan. While some of the recipes are easier if you own accessories, such as the frying basket for the square pan, the accessories are not necessary. For frying, you can just use tongs to remove the food (with caution!) and you will still have incredible, crispy fried chicken or crunchy veggie tempura.

Each of the recipes in *Copper Magic!* has been crafted to take advantage of all that copper pans have to offer. Some are perfect for entertaining large crowds, and others can be just for you. Enjoy the bliss of cooking on the incredible nonstick copper cookware that makes good food every time. As you try the recipes, you can get creative and swap ingredients to make them all your own, too! Most of all, you can enjoy cooking and eating delicious meals that are easy to make and easy to clean up, and that will become fast favorites.

Bon appétit!

Appetizers
AND
Snacks

Spinach and Artichoke Dip

SPINACH AND ARTICHOKE DIP is a party-planning must-have. It's one of those snacks that your guests will come back to again and again, so you should make it count! Serve the dip hot from the oven with an assortment of raw veggies and pita chips.

SERVES: 15-20

2 (14-ounce) cans artichoke hearts, drained and finely chopped

2 (10-ounce) packages frozen chopped spinach, thawed and well-drained

1½ cups grated Parmesan cheese

1½ cups mayonnaise

1 cup shredded mozzarella cheese

1 teaspoon minced garlic or garlic powder

1 teaspoon sambal or your favorite hot sauce

1 teaspoon kosher salt

1 Preheat oven to 350°F. In medium bowl, combine all ingredients. Spoon mixture into lightly greased copper pan.

2 Bake, covered, until heated through and cheese is melted, 20–30 minutes.

Crunchy Potato Skins

NOTHING MAKES A GAME DAY or a backyard barbecue quite like Crunchy Potato Skins. This tasty treat is perfect for any time of year, and requires little to no fuss. If you're in a time crunch, feel free to heat the potatoes in the microwave for a minute before putting them in the oven. Use Greek yogurt instead of sour cream to get that tangy topping flavor without all the fat.

SERVES: 6-8

4 large baking potatoes

3 tablespoons olive oil

½ teaspoon garlic powder

¼ teaspoon paprika

½ teaspoon kosher salt

⅛ teaspoon freshly ground black pepper

8 slices bacon, cooked and crumbled

2 cups shredded Cheddar cheese

½ cup Greek yogurt (optional)

4 scallions, sliced

1   Preheat oven to 375°F. Wash potatoes and place, uncovered, in copper pan. Heat in oven until potatoes are soft all the way through when pierced with a fork, 45-60 minutes. Increase oven temperature to 475°F.

2   Cut potatoes in half lengthwise; scoop out most of the pulp and save for another use, leaving a ¼-inch-thick potato shell.

3   Brush potato shells with oil on all sides and place in single layer in greased, uncovered copper pan, skin-side up. Bake for about 10 minutes. Turn over and sprinkle with garlic powder, paprika, salt, pepper, bacon, and cheese.

4   Bake until cheese is melted, about 5 minutes longer. Top with Greek yogurt, if using, and scallions before serving.

Honey-Chili Chicken Wings

CRUNCHY AND FLAKY FRIED CHICKEN WINGS are not always easy to master, especially when you're loading them up with your favorite sauce. You can get all the crunch by frying them first and tossing them in the sauce right before serving. This recipe has the perfect kick of heat with some sweetness to round it out. It's preferable to use a frying basket while cooking these up, but you can go without—just use caution when removing the wings from the piping-hot oil.

SERVES: 8-10

3 tablespoons canola oil, divided, plus additional for frying

2 red onions, roughly chopped

1 tablespoon minced garlic

2 red or green jalapeños, minced

2 large red bell peppers, seeded and roughly chopped

Kosher salt and freshly ground black pepper

1 cup rice vinegar

¼ cup honey or agave syrup

3 pounds chicken wings

2 tablespoons chopped scallions

Sesame seeds for garnish, if desired

1   Heat copper pan over medium-high heat. Add 1 tablespoon oil and swirl to coat pan. When oil is hot, add onions and garlic and sauté, stirring, for 1 minute. Add jalapeños and bell peppers, season with salt and pepper, and sauté until soft, 4–5 minutes. Add vinegar, stir, and cook until liquid is reduced by half, 2–3 minutes. Transfer mixture to blender and purée, drizzling in agave syrup or honey and remaining 2 tablespoons oil. Season with salt and pepper, and continue to purée until mixture is very smooth. Set aside.

2   Fill clean pan ⅓ of the way with oil and add fryer basket if available. Heat on high until oil reaches 375–400°F.

3 Pat wings dry and season with salt and pepper. Working in batches, if necessary, add wings to pan and fry until crisp and golden brown, 10-15 minutes. Drain wings on paper towels, then transfer them to a large serving bowl. Season with salt and pepper to taste. When all wings are cooked, toss with sauce, reserving some sauce for dipping, if desired.

4 Garnish with scallions and sesame seeds, if desired. Serve with reserved chili sauce.

Pesto-Chicken Spring Rolls

THERE'S NO END TO THE CREATIVITY you can apply to homemade spring rolls. In this recipe, these crunchy-fried appetizers have a tasty kick of garlicky pesto. Make this a fun family activity by rolling the egg roll wrappers as a group. It's OK if they're not shaped perfectly—they'll still taste great!

SERVES: 6-8

1 pound ground chicken breast, cooked

3 cups baby spinach, finely chopped

1 cup shredded carrots

1 pint pesto sauce

Kosher salt and freshly ground black pepper

1 package frozen egg roll wrappers or lumpia wrappers, thawed

Canola oil, for frying

1   Fill a bowl with ice and fill another bowl with the chicken on top of the ice. Add spinach, carrots, and three-quarters of pesto. Mix together. Season with salt and pepper. (If desired, check seasoning by microwaving or sautéing a small portion of the filling.)

2   Lay out egg roll wrappers. Place chicken mixture at one end, then fold wrapper over filling. Continue rolling the wrapper tightly, tucking in the ends as you go, until you've created a roll shape. Let rest seam-side down. Repeat with remaining wrappers.

3   Fill ⅓ of the copper pan with oil and heat on medium-high until oil reaches 350°F. Add egg rolls a few at a time. Place the fryer basket on top of the egg rolls to help keep them immersed in the liquid. Fry until golden brown, 5-7 minutes. Drain on paper towels. Serve with remaining pesto sauce.

Garlic-Cheddar Pick-Apart Bread

ONCE YOU MAKE GARLIC-CHEDDAR PICK-APART BREAD, you'll never go back. The flaky French bread topped with ooey, gooey cheese is easy to make and fun to eat. Cutting a crisscross pattern into the loaf of bread forms finger-friendly cubes that your kids or guests will happily devour. If toppings of garlic and cheese aren't enough, feel free to add other savory additions like crunchy bacon pieces.

SERVES: 4-6

1 large loaf French bread

1 teaspoon garlic powder

1 bunch scallions, sliced

½ cup shredded sharp Cheddar cheese

1 cup shredded mozzarella cheese

1 tablespoon chopped fresh parsley

¼ cup (½ stick) unsalted butter, melted

1   Preheat oven to 350°F. Make 5–7 diagonal slices in the loaf without completely cutting through bottom crust. Then make 5–7 slices in opposite direction, making a checkerboard pattern of bread cubes about 1-inch across.

2   Place bread in copper pan. Sprinkle garlic powder and scallions evenly into slits, then follow with cheeses and parsley. Pour melted butter over top.

3   Cover and bake for 20 minutes. Then uncover and bake for another 10 minutes, until cheese is melted and top of loaf is crispy. Serve while hot.

Crunchy Veggie Tempura

YOU CAN FIND VEGETABLE TEMPURA at many Japanese restaurants, but why not make it at home? This Crunchy Veggie Tempura recipe is easy to make because you're not restricted to certain ingredients. Using whatever fresh vegetables you have on hand, you'll have a tasty, crunchy, battered and fried delight ready to go in minutes.

SERVES: 4-6

1 ⅓ cups cold club soda

2 cups rice flour

Oil for frying

1 tablespoon ground coriander

1 tablespoon paprika

1 teaspoon freshly ground black pepper

2 cups bite-sized raw vegetables like shishito peppers, mushroom caps, zucchini slices and scallions

Kosher salt

1   In large bowl, whisk club soda into rice flour until a pancake-batter consistency is reached. Fold in spices.

2   Fill copper pan ⅓ of the way with oil, add fryer basket if available, and heat on medium-high until oil reaches 350°F.

3   Working in batches, dip the vegetables in the batter and immediately place in oil. Fry vegetables until batter starts to turn golden, 1–3 minutes. Drain on paper towels before serving. Season with salt to taste.

Homemade Potato Chips

THERE'S NOTHING MORE DISAPPOINTING than opening a bag of potato chips only to be greeted with more air than salty snack. Have all the crunchy, crispy, salty potato chips you like when you make them at home! Soak the potato slices before you cook them to remove the extra starch, which will help them fry to the perfect crisp.

SERVES: 6-8

4 medium Russet potatoes, peeled and sliced paper-thin

Water

Peanut or canola oil, for frying

1 tablespoon kosher salt, plus additional for seasoning

1 tablespoon paprika

1   Place potato slices into large bowl of cold water as you slice. Drain, rinse, then refill the bowl with water, and add salt. Let potatoes soak in salty water for at least 30 minutes. Drain, then rinse and drain again. Dry thoroughly with paper towels to prevent splashing.

2   Fill copper pan ⅓ of the way full with oil, add fryer basket if available, and heat on high until oil reaches 365°F.

3   Working in batches if necessary so as to not overfill pan, add potato slices one by one. Fry until they just begin to turn golden, 3-5 minutes. Remove and drain on paper towels. Season with additional salt and paprika.

Sriracha Burger Bites

ENJOY JUICY, FLAVORFUL BURGERS in just a few bites! Alone, burger sliders are the perfect appetizer, and together they're a fun, tasty meal. These Sriracha Burger Bites have a kick of heat for spice lovers, and they can be made even better with garlic rolls instead of buns, or your favorite toppings.

SERVES: 12

1 onion minced

4 cloves garlic, minced

1½ pounds ground beef

1 pound ground pork

1 teaspoon Sriracha or chili powder

12 mini burger buns

3 tablespoons unsalted butter, softened

1 clove garlic, minced

½ pound cheddar cheese, shredded or sliced

Onion slices, tomato slices, and/or pickles for serving

1   Heat oil in copper pan, cook onions, garlic, and meat with the Sriracha or chili powder. Season with salt and pepper to taste and cook through, set aside.

2   Stir together the softened butter and garlic and season with salt and pepper.

3   Preheat the oven to 450°F. Open the package of the slider buns and while keeping them together separate the bottom and top pieces from each other. Lay the bottom buns in one layer in the pan. Spread half of the garlic butter on the bottom half of the buns. Cover the bottom layer of buns with the meat then top with the shredded cheese. Place the top layer of buns over and spread the other half of the butter on the top layer of the buns. Place the pan in the oven until the buns are golden brown and the cheese has melted. Serve with onion slices, tomato slices, and pickles, if desired.

Goat Cheese & Bacon Dates

A LITTLE BIT OF SWEETNESS, a little bit of cheesiness, and a whole lot of bacon make these bite-sized treats oh-so-good. The rich flavor combination and petite size make these the perfect finger food for parties. Use thinly sliced bacon to ensure that it'll crisp up just right. If you want to switch things up a bit, you can use blue cheese instead of goat cheese.

SERVES: 10-12

20 dates

6 ounces goat cheese

1 (16-ounce) package bacon

1 teaspoon coriander

1   Preheat oven to 350°F. Slice dates open on one side and remove pit. Stuff approximately 1 teaspoon goat cheese into the cavity of each date and press sides together to close. Cut bacon slices in half and wrap each date with a slice of bacon. Secure with a toothpick.

2   Place dates in single layer in copper pan and sprinkle with coriander. Bake until bacon is browned, 8–10 minutes, then turn and continue to bake, until all sides are browned, 10–12 minutes more.

3   Drain on paper towels and let cool for several minutes before serving.

Must-Have BBQ Meatballs

YOU JUST UPPED YOUR APPETIZER GAME. These tangy, garlicky meatballs are the perfect addition to any backyard party or pot-luck. Rolling them into smaller, bite-sized balls will make them easier to pop in your mouth and satisfy that hunger.

SERVES: 10-12

BARBECUE SAUCE

2 cups ketchup

¾ cup chicken stock or water

½ cup apple cider vinegar

¼ cup packed dark brown sugar

¼ cup granulated sugar

1 tablespoon honey mustard

1 tablespoon Worcestershire sauce

2 teaspoons garlic powder

1 teaspoon onion powder

1 teaspoon kosher salt

1 teaspoon freshly ground black pepper

1   In copper pan, combine all ingredients and bring to a boil over medium-high heat.

2   Reduce heat to low and simmer, uncovered, stirring approximately every 15 minutes, until thickened and reduced to approximately 2 cups, about 1 hour. Transfer sauce to a separate container and set aside.

MEATBALLS

1 pound ground beef

½ pound ground pork

1 large onion, finely chopped

¾ cup panko (Japanese bread crumbs)

1 egg, lightly beaten

½ cup milk

1 teaspoon sambal or cayenne pepper

1½ teaspoons kosher salt

½ teaspoon freshly ground black pepper

1   Preheat oven to 350°F. Loosely mix together all ingredients. Shape into balls approximately ¾ inch to 1 inch in diameter and place in single layer in clean copper pan.

2   Pour 1½ cups barbecue sauce over meatballs and bake, covered, for 30 minutes. Top with remaining sauce and bake uncovered until cooked through, 10-15 minutes more.

Hearty Breakfasts

Garden-Fresh Frittata

MAKE THE MOST OF FRESH VEGETABLES with a Garden-Fresh Frittata! Great for Saturday morning breakfast with family, or to make at the beginning of the week for your daily breakfast, this frittata incorporates delicious, healthy vegetables with cheesy, protein-filled egg goodness. If you don't have all of these veggies on hand, feel free to swap them out for whatever you have in the fridge.

SERVES: 4-6

1 teaspoon olive oil

½ summer squash, chopped into half moons

½ cup zucchini, chopped into half moons

½ cup Baby Bella mushrooms, chopped

½ medium red pepper, julienned

¼ teaspoon garlic powder

Kosher salt and freshly ground black pepper

10 eggs

¼ cup whole milk

½ cup sharp Cheddar cheese, grated

10 cherry tomatoes, halved

1 stalk green onion, chopped

1   Preheat oven to 375°F. In a saucepan, sauté the summer squash, zucchini, mushrooms and red pepper in olive oil. Add garlic powder and season with salt and pepper. Cook until barely soft.

2   Combine eggs and milk in a bowl and whisk until frothy. Season lightly with salt and pepper.

3   Poor egg mixture into a preheated copper pan and cook on medium to high heat until it sets, stirring as necessary. Place in the oven for 10 minutes until the top has set and the eggs are no longer liquid.

4   Remove from oven and sprinkle with cheese and all of the vegetable mixture, plus cherry tomatoes. Return to oven and cook for another 10 to 12 minutes. Garnish with green onion and serve from the copper pan.

Classic Chocolate Chip Pancakes

PANCAKES ARE A WEEKEND STAPLE, but sometimes they can be a hassle when you don't have the right cooking surface. The square copper pan removes all of this frustration, giving you enough space to cook multiple pancakes at once! Sprinkle in chocolate chips or your go-to pancake ingredient, such as bananas, blueberries, or cinnamon.

SERVES: 4-6

1 cup all-purpose flour

1 tablespoon sugar

2 teaspoons baking powder

⅛ teaspoon kosher salt

1 large egg

1 cup 2% milk

2 tablespoons canola oil

1 cup chocolate chips

1 In medium bowl, combine flour, sugar, baking powder, and salt.

2 In separate medium bowl, add egg, milk, and oil and whisk to combine well.

3 Make an indentation in the middle of flour mixture, then pour in egg mixture and mix until incorporated and lumps just start to disappear. Fold in chocolate chips.

4 Heat a lightly greased copper pan over medium heat. Pour about ¼ cup batter per pancake into pan, making 3-4 pancakes each batch. Flip when bubbles in batter start to pop, about 2 minutes. Cook on other side until both sides are golden brown, about 2 minutes more. Serve with butter and maple syrup, if desired.

Raspberry Jam Breakfast Croissants

THE MOST SCRUMPTIOUS FOODS don't have to be hard work. With a package of crescent rolls, you can have delicious, buttery and sweet Raspberry Jam Breakfast Croissants that smell and taste like they came from your local bakery. If raspberry isn't your jam, feel free to swap for other fruit, jam, or jelly of your choosing.

SERVES: 6-8

1 (8-ounce) package refrigerated crescent dinner rolls

¼ cup raspberry jam or jelly or your favorite fruit

1 tablespoon unsalted butter, melted

Sesame seeds, if desired

1   Preheat oven to 375°F. Separate dough into 8 triangles. Spread each triangle with jam, then roll up loosely into crescent roll shape, starting at the shortest side of the triangle and rolling to the opposite point.

2   Place croissants in ungreased copper pan. Brush with melted butter. Sprinkle with sesame seeds, if desired. Bake, uncovered, until golden, 11–13 minutes.

Breakfast on a Biscuit

WHATEVER YOUR BREAKFAST SANDWICH FANCY—be it ham, bacon, turkey bacon, or just plain egg and cheese—a buttery biscuit sandwich warmed up in a copper pan might be the very best way to start your day. To make meals stretch, bake a batch of store-bought biscuits for dinner one night, and use the leftovers (if you have any!) for this sandwich in the morning.

SERVES: 1

2 teaspoons unsalted butter, separated

1 large egg

1 thick slice ham or other meat

½ slice Cheddar or American cheese

1 biscuit, sliced in half

1 Heat 1 teaspoon of butter in copper pan over medium-high heat. Once melted, break egg and carefully slip it into one corner of pan, then immediately reduce heat to low. Cook until white is completely set and yolk begins to thicken, about 1 minute.

2 Meanwhile, heat ham slice in other corner of copper pan until hot, flipping halfway through, 30–60 seconds.

3 In another corner of the pan, add the second teaspoon of butter and split the biscuit. Place in the melted butter and griddle until hot.

4 Place cheese on bottom half of biscuit, followed by egg, ham, and biscuit top. Serve.

Classic French Toast Sticks

TO MAKE THE PERFECT FRENCH TOAST, you'll want to use thick-cut bread that is just a little bit stale. Leave the bread you'll be using out the night before with a paper towel on top, and in the morning, you'll have the perfect bread for Classic French Toast Sticks. This breakfast treat will absorb all of the tasty flavors, without sacrificing texture.

SERVES: 4

4 large eggs

1 cup heavy cream

2 teaspoons cinnamon

1 tablespoon sugar

⅛ teaspoon kosher salt

1 tablespoon vanilla extract

2-3 tablespoons unsalted butter

8 thick slices (such as Texas-toast style) crusty bread, cut into 4 strips

Powdered sugar, for dusting

Maple syrup, for serving

1 In large bowl, whisk together eggs, cream, cinnamon, sugar, salt, and vanilla. Set aside.

2 Heat copper pan over medium heat and add butter. While butter is melting, coat half the French toast sticks in the egg mixture by dipping and turning until soaked through.

3 Place coated sticks in a single layer in pan. Cook, flipping halfway through, until golden brown on both sides, about 5 minutes total.

4 Dust with powdered sugar and serve with maple syrup and fresh fruit.

Tea-Time Donuts

IF YOU THOUGHT THAT COFFEE is a donut's only breakfast companion or that potatoes had no place in your sweets, you'd be wrong on both counts. This recipe uses mashed potatoes as a primary ingredient to make extra fluffy donuts, with the flavors of a strong tea like Earl Grey to make a memorable donut feast. Drizzle with chocolate sauce or sprinkle with sugar for an anytime treat.

SERVES: 6-8

½ cup milk

1 (¼-ounce) packet active dry yeast (2¼ teaspoons)

¼ cup strong tea

¼ cup plus 2 tablespoons corn syrup

1 large egg

3¼ cups all-purpose flour plus more for dusting

¼ cup (½ stick) cold unsalted butter, cut into 1-inch cubes

¼ cup mashed potatoes (leftover or prepared instant)

½ teaspoon kosher salt

¼ cup chocolate syrup plus more for drizzling

Oil for frying

1   In a standing mixer with the paddle attachment, combine milk and yeast. Add remaining ingredients except chocolate syrup, in order, and, on low speed, mix until well incorporated, about 5 minutes. Increase speed to medium to further work the dough, being careful not to overwork. You are looking for the dough to become shiny and, when you pull off a piece and stretch it with your hands, it should be very pliable.

2   Place dough in large, lightly greased bowl and let rise at room temperature, covered, until doubled in volume, 1½–2 hours.

3   Turn dough out onto a lightly floured surface and fold it over onto itself. Knead until smooth and roll out ½-inch thick. Cut dough into 1-inch strips, then form into rounds. Let rise, covered with a towel, in a warm place for 30 minutes.

4   Fill copper pan halfway with oil, add fryer basket if available, and heat on high until oil reaches 365°F. Working in batches, add donuts 2 or 3 at a time and fry until golden brown, about 3 minutes, flipping halfway through. Remove and drain on paper towels. Season with additional kosher salt and drizzle with chocolate syrup before serving.

Egg Scramble on Avocado Toast

AVOCADO TOAST IS ONE OF THOSE SPECIAL BREAKFAST GEMS that can take a multitude of forms. Sometimes a little bit of olive oil and sea salt with smashed avocado is just enough, and other times you need a hearty meal to get your day going. The best part about Egg Scramble on Avocado Toast is that you can modify it to meet your tastes—make it with wheat, grain, or even pumpernickel bread, or add some hot sauce to kick it up a notch!

SERVES: 1-2

2 slices wheat bread

3 large eggs

3 tablespoons milk

1 avocado, sliced

8 cherry tomatoes, halved for serving

Lime juice

Kosher salt and freshly ground black pepper

1   Heat copper pan over medium heat. Add bread to corner of pan.

2   Meanwhile, beat together eggs and milk. Pour mixture into the other corner of the pan and immediately stir to scramble the eggs until cooked.

3   Flip bread when bottom begins to brown and continue to cook until both sides have browned. Remove bread from pan.

4   Place bread on plate. Top with eggs, avocado and tomatoes. Sprinkle on lime juice and season to taste with salt and pepper.

Morning Cinnamon Buns

NOTHING SMELLS OF COMFORT AND HOME quite like fresh cinnamon buns. With this recipe, you can bring the aroma of freshly baked buns to your guests or family any time! To add a little extra flavor, swap out the cinnamon for ground five spice. If you're big on the classic glazed cinnamon buns, drizzle some warm icing over these for an exceptional morning treat.

SERVES: 4-6

1 cup 2% milk

3 tablespoons unsalted butter

1 (¼-ounce) packet instant or rapid rise yeast (2¼ teaspoons)

¼ cup plus 1 tablespoon sugar, divided

¼ teaspoon kosher salt

3 cups all-purpose flour, plus more for dusting

2 teaspoons canola oil, for coating

¼ cup (½ stick) unsalted butter, melted

2 teaspoons ground five spice or cinnamon

1   In small copper pan or saucepan, heat milk and 3 tablespoons butter over medium-low heat until warm but not scalding, about 110°F. Remove from heat. (If you overheat it, let it cool down to 110°F before using, so it doesn't kill the yeast.) Sprinkle yeast on top and let sit, covered, for 10 minutes. Stir in 1 tablespoon sugar and salt.

2   Transfer mixture to large bowl and add flour, ½ cup at a time, stirring as you go (you may not need all of it).

3   When dough is too thick to stir but still sticky, transfer to a lightly floured surface and knead until it forms a loose ball, 1-2 minutes (be careful not to overmix). Rinse mixing bowl, coat with canola oil, then add dough ball back in. Cover with plastic wrap and set in a warm place to rise for about 1 hour, or until doubled in size.

4   On a lightly floured surface, roll out dough into thin rectangle. Brush with 2 tablespoons melted butter and top with cinnamon and remaining sugar.

5   Starting at one end, tightly roll up dough and lay seam-side down. Then with a serrated knife, cut dough into 1-inch sections and place cut-side up in a well-greased copper pan. Brush with remaining melted butter and cover with plastic wrap. Let rise again while you preheat oven to 350°F.

6   Once oven is hot, bake rolls for 25–30 minutes, or until just golden brown. Let cool for a few minutes before serving.

Lunch Favorites

Mini Calzones with Ham & Mozzarella

MAKE TONIGHT CALZONE NIGHT! This recipe calls for ham, but you can swap ham out for another ingredient like sausage, chicken, pepperoni, or even your favorite veggies. Folding the scallions into the pizza dough makes for an even tastier experience. Serve this with a side of warmed marinara sauce for dipping.

SERVES: 4-8

1 pound ham, chopped

1½ cups shredded mozzarella cheese

¼ teaspoon dried oregano

¼ teaspoon dried basil

½ teaspoon garlic powder

⅛ teaspoon cayenne pepper

½ teaspoon kosher salt

¼ teaspoon freshly ground black pepper

1 (16-ounce) package refrigerated pizza dough

1 bunch scallions, sliced

1 large egg, beaten

Pizza sauce or marinara sauce, for serving

1   Preheat oven to 375°F. In medium bowl, combine ham, cheese, oregano, basil, garlic powder, cayenne, salt, and black pepper. Stir to combine.

2   Fold scallions into the pizza dough until well incorporated. Divide into 8 sections and roll into balls, then flatten each ball into a circle, about ¼- to ½-inch thick. Place meat mixture onto one half of each of circle, leaving a ½-inch border around the edge. Fold dough over filling, then press edges of dough together with tines of a fork to seal.

3   Place mini calzones on lightly greased copper pan and brush tops with egg. Prick tops with fork to allow steam to escape.

4   Bake uncovered for 20-22 minutes or until dough is golden brown. Cool 10 minutes on cooling rack. Serve with warmed marinara sauce.

Flaky Biscuit Pizzas

MAKE-AT-HOME PIZZAS ARE A FUN WAY to put dinner on the table—there are no rules for how they should look or what kinds of toppings should be on them—the creativity is endless! With Flaky Biscuit Pizzas, you can use a tube of flaky biscuit rounds, press them flat to make your pizza base, and then go wild with your favorite toppings. This recipe makes a classic margherita, but you can make it all your own.

SERVES: 4-6

2 rounds refrigerated flaky biscuit dough

1 bunch scallions, sliced

¼ cup pizza sauce

1 cup fresh mozzarella cheese, shredded

1 tomato, cut crosswise

1 tablespoon chopped fresh basil

1   Preheat oven to 375°F. Roll out the biscuit dough into 6-inch rounds. Press the sliced scallions into each round. Place on greased copper pan. Top each round with pizza sauce, cheese, and tomato.

2   Bake for 10-15 minutes, or until bottoms are deep golden brown and cheese is bubbly. Top with fresh basil before serving.

Balsamic White Bean Toast

HEALTHY AND EXCEPTIONALLY TASTY, this twist on toast will be your new favorite. Choose a fresh, flavorful loaf of bread like ciabatta or focaccia as the canvas for this lunchtime masterpiece. Topped with tomatoes, hearty cannellini beans, and a dash of tangy balsamic vinegar, this lunch is a zesty and nutritious way to satisfy those hunger pangs.

SERVES: 6-8

- 1 tablespoon olive oil
- 1 onion, finely chopped
- 4 cloves garlic, minced
- 1 tablespoon fermented black bean paste, minced
- 1 teaspoon smoked paprika
- 2 tablespoons balsamic vinegar
- 2 (14-ounce) cans cannellini beans, mostly drained
- 1 (14.5-ounce) can petite-cut tomatoes
- 1 teaspoon Worcestershire sauce
- ⅛ teaspoon cayenne pepper (optional)
- Kosher salt and freshly ground black pepper
- 8 thick slices artisan bread
- 2 teaspoons fresh thyme leaves, for garnish

1   Preheat oven to 325°F. Add oil to copper pan, and heat over medium heat. Add onion, garlic, fermented black beans and paprika. Cook, covered, stirring occasionally, until onions are soft, 3–5 minutes. Add vinegar and beans and stir to combine well. Add tomatoes, Worcestershire sauce, and cayenne pepper, if using. Season well with salt and black pepper and continue cooking for another 5 minutes.

2   Transfer copper pan to preheated oven and bake for 40–50 minutes, until mixture is thick.

3   Toast the bread, then divide beans among the slices. Season with salt to taste and sprinkle with thyme. Serve hot.

Ginger–Kiwi Chicken Quesadillas

QUESADILLAS MIGHT AS WELL BE THEIR OWN FOOD GROUP, because you can mix, match, and modify any quesadilla to make it all your own. The standout to this recipe is the salsa. Spicy ginger, sweet kiwi, and cooling jicama all chopped and tossed together make this chicken quesadilla recipe a soon-to-be household favorite. For best results, use a large pan and cook the quesadillas in batches.

SERVES: 4

QUESADILLAS

4 flour tortillas
(8-inch diameter)

2 teaspoons olive oil

1½ cups shredded
Monterey Jack cheese

2 cups chopped
cooked chicken

2 tablespoons
chopped cilantro

1   Place copper pan over medium heat. Working in batches, brush tortillas with olive oil on one side, and place 1 tortilla olive-oil-side down in pan. Spread quesadilla ingredients evenly over tortillas and top with another tortilla olive-oil-side up.

2   Cook until golden on each side. Remove and serve with salsa.

SALSA

1 tablespoon minced ginger

4 kiwis, peeled and cut into ¼-inch dice

2 cups ¼-inch-dice jicama

1 cup ¼-inch-dice red onion

¼ cup packed chopped cilantro

1 jalapeño, stemmed and minced with seeds

Juice of 4 limes

2 ounces agave tequila

Kosher salt and freshly ground black pepper

Sugar

1   In large bowl, gently mix all salsa ingredients. Season with salt, pepper, and sugar to taste. Let stand at room temperature for at least an hour, or covered overnight in the refrigerator before using.

Crispy Bacon Grilled Cheese

MAKE PERFECTLY GRILLED, BUTTERY AND GOOEY GRILLED CHEESE on your copper pan. If you're cooking for a crowd, use the square copper pan so you can make four at once! Add your favorite grilled cheese ingredients, like bacon, avocado, or tomato. The pan will brown these sandwiches to perfection.

SERVES: 4

8 slices firm sandwich bread

2–3 tablespoons mayonnaise

8 slices Cheddar or American cheese

8 slices crisply cooked bacon, halved

1   Heat copper pan over medium-low heat. Spread mayo evenly over one side of each bread slice. Place 4 slices bread, mayo-side down, in copper pan.

2   Place cheese and bacon on top of bread; top with remaining bread, mayo-side up. Cook 3 minutes per side or until golden brown and cheese is melted. Cut sandwiches diagonally into halves before serving.

Homemade Chicken Fingers

THERE'S NO NEED TO ORDER TAKEOUT when you can make crispy chicken fingers right at home. With the deep square copper pan, frying is easy, and they'll taste so much better because you made them yourself. If you want to take things one step further, you can toss the finished products with some buffalo sauce or honey mustard just before serving.

SERVES: 4

½ cup all-purpose flour

1 teaspoon onion powder

1 teaspoon paprika

2 large eggs, beaten

1 cup panko (Japanese bread crumbs)

2 large boneless, skinless chicken breast halves, cut into long strips

Kosher salt and freshly ground black pepper

Canola oil, for frying

Chopped chives, for garnish (optional)

1   Mix flour with spices. Place flour and spice mix, egg and panko in three separate bowls.

2   Season chicken slices with salt and pepper, then dredge in flour, then dip in egg, letting excess drip off. Next, dip in panko, covering thoroughly.

3   Fill ⅓ of the copper pan with oil and heat over high heat; add fryer basket if available. Heat until oil reaches 375°F, then place chicken strips in pan and cook until golden brown, 10-12 minutes. Remove and season lightly with salt and pepper. Garnish with chives, if using.

Croque Monsieur

THE FRENCHMAN'S HAM AND CHEESE is indulgent, delicious, and hard to pass up. Rather than grilling this up with butter, the rich white sauce coats the Croque Monsieur for one incredible sandwich experience. This is perfect for a cold winter day or one of those times when no food but comfort food will do.

SERVES: 2

1 tablespoon unsalted butter

1 tablespoon all-purpose flour

1 cup milk, warmed

Kosher salt

Grated nutmeg

4 slices thick country bread (not sourdough or whole wheat)

4 slices ham

4 slices Gruyère or Monterey Jack cheese

1 Preheat oven to 300°F. In small saucepan over medium heat, melt 1 tablespoon butter. When bubbles have subsided, remove from heat, add flour, and whisk vigorously until well combined. Return to heat, add warm milk, and cook, stirring continuously, until sauce thickens, 3–5 minutes. Remove from heat, and season to taste with salt and nutmeg.

2 Spread slices of bread generously with sauce. Lay the ham and a slice of cheese on top of two of the slices. The ham and cheese should slightly overlap edges of bread. Top each with a slice of bread, and then top each sandwich with the remaining slices of cheese.

3 Preheat copper pan on top of stove on medium for about 5 minutes. Place sandwiches cheese-side down and cook on stovetop until bottom bread slice starts to brown and bubble, then flip sandwiches and transfer copper pan to oven. Bake until heated through and cheese is bubbling, 5–10 minutes. Serve hot.

Butternut Squash Soup with Ginger

THE BEST PART OF THIS SOUP is that to make it just right, it requires you to fill your home with the aromas of slowly baked squash, fresh ginger, and cinnamon. If you're tight on time, you can microwave the squash and skip to the second step. Use a deep copper pan to bring all those delicious autumn flavors together for a comforting seasonal soup.

SERVES: 4-6

2 butternut squash, halved

2 tablespoons vegetable oil

2 cups thinly sliced onion

1 tablespoon light brown sugar

2 tablespoons minced fresh ginger

2 cloves garlic, coarsely chopped

½ cinnamon stick

5 cups (or more) low-sodium chicken stock

Kosher salt and freshly ground black pepper

2 tablespoons plain yogurt

1 tablespoon chopped fresh cilantro

1   Preheat oven to 375°F. Place squash on greased copper pan. Bake until squash is very soft, about 50 minutes, turning halfway through. Discard seeds and peel and cut squash into 2-inch cubes.

2   Heat oil in clean copper pan over medium-low heat. Add onion and stir, then cover and cook until onion is tender, 10-15 minutes, stirring once or twice during cooking time. Add squash, brown sugar, ginger, garlic, cinnamon, and 5 cups chicken stock. Season with salt and pepper to taste. Bring to boil. Reduce heat to medium-low. Cover and simmer 10 minutes. Discard cinnamon.

3   Working in batches, purée soup in blender. Return soup to pan. Bring to simmer, thinning soup with more broth if necessary. Ladle into bowls. Drizzle each bowl with yogurt and sprinkle with cilantro before serving.

Light Soba Noodle Soup

SOBA NOODLE SOUP IS A DELICIOUS AND SATISFYING SOUP that won't weigh you down. The crisp, light broth packs a lot of flavor, and with the added Cucumber-Wasabi Salad on top, you'll have just the right balance of heat. You can find sake for the broth in wine or liquor stores.

SERVES: 3-4

SOUP

1 (8- to 9-ounce) package soba noodles

1 tablespoon canola oil

2 large onions, thinly sliced

Kosher salt and freshly ground black pepper

1 cup sake

2 tablespoons soy sauce

1 teaspoon toasted sesame oil

2 quarts low-sodium vegetable stock

2 tablespoons chopped scallions

1   Fill a large bowl with water and add ice. Boil water in copper pan, then add noodles and abundant salt. Cook until al dente, about 7 minutes. Drain and transfer to bowl of ice water. When noodles are cold, drain well and set aside.

2   Heat copper pan over medium-high heat. Add 1 tablespoon canola oil and swirl to coat the bottom. When oil is hot, add onions, season with salt and pepper, and cook, stirring once, until caramelized, 10–12 minutes. Add sake, and scrape bottom of pan to incorporate brown bits. Add soy sauce, sesame oil, and stock and bring to a simmer. Add noodles and heat through. Divide soup among 4 bowls. Make a mound of noodles in each, and top with scallions or cucumber salad before serving.

CUCUMBER-WASABI SALAD

1 heaping teaspoon wasabi powder mixed with 1 tablespoon room-temperature water

1 tablespoon soy sauce

1 small English cucumber, very thinly sliced

1 tablespoon canola oil

1 tablespoon toasted sesame seeds

1   In medium bowl, combine wasabi, soy sauce, cucumber slices, and canola oil. Add half of sesame seeds and toss.

Garnish with remaining sesame seeds before serving.

Potato-Leek & Bacon Soup

A WARMING WINTER TREAT, Potato-Leek & Bacon Soup is as comforting as it is delicious. With hearty potatoes, flavorful leeks, and crispy bacon, this is one recipe you won't want to forget. To reduce some of the cook time, feel free to microwave the potatoes instead of roasting them. Use a deep copper pan to cook the soup to perfection.

SERVES: 4-6

3 medium white potatoes

6 slices bacon

1 large white onion, finely chopped

2 large leeks

2 cups chicken stock

1 tablespoon minced garlic

3 cups 2% milk

1 teaspoon kosher salt

1 teaspoon freshly ground black pepper

¼ cup chopped onion, for garnish

2 teaspoons chopped fresh thyme, for garnish

1 Preheat oven to 400°F. Pierce potatoes and bake in the copper pan until tender, about 45-60 minutes.

2 When potatoes are cool enough to handle, peel them. Mash the potatoes with a potato masher.

3 Place bacon in clean copper pan, then heat to medium-low. Cook, flipping once, 8-12 minutes, or until cooked through and edges start to curl. Remove bacon to paper towels to drain. Crumble when cool. Set aside. Don't drain the pan; keep the fat in it to use.

4 Raise heat to medium-high and add onion, leeks and garlic. Stir occasionally for 3-5 minutes. Add stock, mashed potatoes, milk, salt and pepper. Bring mixture to a simmer over medium heat, stirring occasionally, about 5 minutes, until soup has thickened slightly.

5 Garnish with bacon to serve.

Dinners
AND
Sides

Mango-Jerk Chicken

EMBRACE THE HEAT OF THIS SPICY JERK RUB! By marinating the chicken for a full day, you'll lock in all of the delicious flavors of the jerk rub, and using bone-in meat will keep the chicken nice and juicy. The caramelized mangoes offer a sweet and cooling balance to the spicy chicken, making this dish a win-win.

SERVES: 8-10

6 cloves garlic

2 tablespoons minced ginger

2 tablespoons minced fresh thyme

2 tablespoons five-spice powder

1 tablespoon freshly ground black pepper

2 tablespoons sambal or 1 small habanero chili, minced

Juice and zest of 1 large orange

2 tablespoons dark brown sugar, divided

1 tablespoon kosher salt

¼ cup grapeseed or canola oil

4-5 pounds chicken legs and thighs

2 mangoes, peeled and cut into wedges

Juice of 1 lime

1   Make marinade a day in advance: Using a mortar and pestle or small food processor, combine garlic, ginger, thyme, five-spice powder, black pepper, sambal, orange zest, 1 tablespoon brown sugar, and salt and blend into a paste. Add orange juice and oil and combine.

2   Coat chicken with jerk paste and marinate overnight, covered, in the refrigerator.

3   The next day, preheat oven to 325°F. In small bowl, combine mangoes, remaining brown sugar, and lime juice. Toss to coat.

4   Heat copper pan over medium-high heat. Remove chicken from marinade and add to pan in batches. Cook until brown on all sides.

5   Return all chicken to the pan and transfer to the oven, covered and heat until chicken is cooked through, about 45–60 minutes. About 20 minutes before chicken is done, add mangoes to pan, and cook until caramelized.

6   Transfer chicken to a cutting board and allow to rest for several minutes. Transfer to a platter, surrounded with caramelized mangoes, and serve.

Roasted Chicken & Honey-Ginger Sweet Potatoes

A SIMPLE STEP TO MAKING succulent roasted chicken is to brine it overnight. The brine is just a simple blend of salt, sugar, and warm water, which marinates the chicken so that it's juicier and more flavorful. Perfectly prepared chicken in combination with Honey-Ginger Sweet Potatoes makes for one fantastic meal.

SERVES: 4-6

⅓ cup kosher salt, for brining, plus more for seasoning

⅓ cup sugar, for brining

8 cups water, for brining

1 whole chicken (4 to 6 pounds)

3 tablespoons olive oil, divided

2 tablespoons minced garlic

2 tablespoons minced fresh thyme, divided

Freshly ground black pepper

1 tablespoon minced ginger

2 tablespoons honey or agave syrup

3 large sweet potatoes, peeled and cut into 1-inch pieces

1 bunch scallions, white and green parts, thinly sliced

1 The night before, brine the chicken: In a large pitcher, combine salt, sugar, and water; stir to dissolve. Put chicken in a bowl or pot large enough to hold it and the brine and pour brine over chicken. If chicken isn't covered, make more brine and add to bowl. Refrigerate overnight. The next day, rinse chicken and pat dry.

2 Preheat oven to 500°F, and place empty copper pan on middle oven rack.

3 Combine olive oil, garlic and 1 tablespoon thyme. Rub all over the inside and outside of the chicken. Season with salt and pepper both inside and outside.

4 In large bowl, combine ginger, honey, sweet potatoes, scallions, remaining 1 tablespoon oil and remaining 1 tablespoon of thyme. Mix well and season with salt and pepper.

5 Pull out the oven rack with the hot pan on it and add potato mixture, which will sizzle. Top with chicken, breast-side up, and roast for 15 minutes. Lower oven temperature to 375°F and continue to roast, rotating pan once, and stirring potatoes halfway through cook time, until the chicken is done, 1¼ hours or until it registers 160°F on a meat thermometer. (If chicken browns too quickly, tent it with foil. Remove the tent 10 minutes before chicken is finished so the skin crisps.)

6 Transfer chicken to a cutting board to rest for 10 minutes. Transfer sweet potatoes to a platter. Place chicken on top of potatoes, spoon pan juices over chicken, and serve.

One-Pot Chicken and Peas

THIS ONE-POT WONDER makes cooking and clean up super easy! With chicken that's simmered in fragrant garlic, and sauce that's thickened with yogurt to make it nice and creamy, this recipe is perfect to serve over your favorite rice, pasta, or even roasted potatoes.

SERVES: 2-4

2 tablespoons olive oil

3-4 boneless, skinless chicken breasts

2 cloves garlic, thinly sliced

1 bunch scallions, chopped

1½ cups chicken stock, warmed

1 (13-ounce) package frozen peas

½ cup plain Greek yogurt

2 tablespoon chopped fresh parsley

1   Add oil to copper pan and heat over medium heat. Season chicken with salt and pepper then add to the pan and brown for 4 minutes per side.

2   Push chicken to one side of pan and add garlic and scallions, cooking for about 30 seconds, until fragrant. Pour in chicken stock, cover, and simmer for 15 minutes.

3   Increase heat to medium-high. Add peas and cook for 5 minutes, covered, until tender. Check to make sure the chicken is cooked through. Turn the heat off and stir in the Greek yogurt. Serve over pasta or rice. Garnish with parsley.

Chicken Sausage and Fennel Rice Medley

THE SMELL AND TASTE OF FENNEL are frequently compared to licorice. While there is a hint of a similarity when fennel is raw, the cooked variety is much subtler and adds a wonderful flavor to many dishes. In this case, the fennel, bell pepper, onions, and celery all work together to make the chicken sausage taste even better.

SERVES: 3-4

2 tablespoons grapeseed or canola oil

1½ pounds chicken sausage

2 medium onions, chopped

1 red bell pepper, chopped

3 fennel bulbs, halved, cored, and sliced ¼-inch thick

3 celery stalks, chopped

Kosher salt and freshly ground black pepper

2 cups jasmine rice, or 1 cup jasmine and 1 cup brown rice

3 cups low-sodium chicken stock

1   Preheat oven to 375°F. Heat copper pan over high heat, add oil, and swirl to coat the bottom. When oil is hot, add sausage and sauté until brown, 6-8 minutes, flipping halfway through. Transfer sausage to a cutting board and let sit for several minutes before slicing.

2   Reduce heat to medium. Add onions, bell pepper, fennel, and celery and season with salt and pepper. Sauté, stirring, until browned, about 8 minutes.

3   Add rice, stir to combine and return sliced sausage to pan. Add stock and season with salt and pepper to taste. Bring to a simmer, cover and transfer pan to the oven. Bake until rice is cooked, about 40 minutes. Remove pan from oven and let stand, covered, for 15 minutes. Serve directly from pan or transfer mixture to a platter and serve.

Buttermilk Fried Chicken

THERE'S NOTHING QUITE LIKE CHOWING DOWN on some crispy fried chicken. Using buttermilk is always a direct route to that crispy, flaky, savory fried coating, while the dose of hot sauce adds just the right amount of flavor. The crunchy outside makes for juicy, flavorful chicken.

SERVES: 3-4

2 large eggs

1 cup buttermilk

1-2 tablespoons sambal or hot sauce

2 cups all-purpose flour

2 teaspoons kosher salt

1½ teaspoons freshly ground black pepper

¼ teaspoon paprika

Vegetable or canola oil, for frying

1 (3- to 4-pound) chicken, cut into 10 pieces

1   In large bowl, whisk eggs, buttermilk, and hot sauce. In separate large bowl, whisk flour, salt, pepper, and paprika.

2   Fill ⅓ of the copper pan with oil and heat over medium-high heat until oil reaches 325°F. Add fryer basket if available.

3   Pat chicken dry and season with salt and pepper. Working with 1 piece at a time, dredge chicken in flour mixture, then in buttermilk mixture, then again in flour mixture.

4   Working in batches and returning oil to 325°F between batches, fry chicken, turning occasionally, until skin is crispy and is golden brown, 15–18 minutes. Transfer to paper towels to drain. Season with salt and pepper to taste.

Rosemary Roasted Chicken and Vegetables

ROASTING A WHOLE CHICKEN AT HOME is one of those special dinners that fills your house with incredible aromas, tastes amazing, and requires almost no effort. This blend of leeks, carrots, potatoes, and celery is classic, but feel free to use whatever vegetables you may have on hand. Consider tossing in a whole head of garlic, top sliced off, for extra flavor.

SERVES: 3-4

1 whole chicken (3½ to 4 pounds), patted dry

Kosher salt and freshly ground black pepper

10 sprigs thyme

5 sprigs rosemary

2 leeks (white and light green parts only), chopped

3 medium carrots, chopped

4 ribs of celery, chopped

2 large sweet potatoes or Yukon gold potatoes

2 teaspoons extra-virgin olive oil

½ cup dry white wine

1 tablespoon chopped fresh parsley

1   Preheat oven to 450°F. Season chicken inside and out with salt and pepper and place in copper pan. Stuff thyme and rosemary into cavity. In a large bowl, toss leeks, carrots, celery and potatoes with oil; season with salt and pepper. Scatter vegetables around chicken, and pour wine into pan.

2   Roast uncovered until chicken is golden brown and cooked through, about an hour (less if you're using a V-rack). Let rest for 10 minutes before carving. Toss vegetables with parsley before serving.

Lemony Chicken Piccata

LEMON AND CHICKEN ARE A MATCH MADE IN HEAVEN, and chicken piccata is one of those classic dishes that should become a household staple. The pounded-out chicken makes for quick cooking, and the all-in-one-pan method helps the chicken absorb the buttery goodness of the lemon–white wine sauce. Serve this dish with steamed veggies or over your favorite pasta.

SERVES: 2

2 boneless, skinless chicken breast halves (8 to 9 ounces each), pounded ¼-inch thick

Kosher salt and freshly ground black pepper

½ cup all-purpose flour

1 tablespoon vegetable or canola oil

3 tablespoons unsalted butter, divided

2 tablespoons minced shallot

3 tablespoons finely chopped parsley stems

¼ cup dry white wine

Juice of 2 lemons (3–4 tablespoons)

¼ cup chicken stock

2 tablespoons capers, drained

1 tablespoon chopped fresh parsley

1   Season chicken on both sides with salt and pepper. Place flour in shallow dish and dredge chicken in it. Shake off excess.

2   In copper pan over medium-high heat, heat oil. Place chicken in pan and cook, turning once, until browned on both sides, 5–6 minutes. Remove chicken from pan.

3   Reduce heat to medium and melt
1 tablespoon butter in pan. Add shallot
and cook until softened and golden
brown, about 30 seconds. Add wine,
lemon juice, and stock, increase heat to
medium-high, and cook until liquid is
slightly reduced, about 5 minutes.

4   Remove pan from heat and whisk in
remaining 2 tablespoons butter, capers,
and parsley. Season with salt and pepper.
Drizzle sauce over chicken.

Curry Chicken with Mediterranean Orzo

PACKED WITH THE FLAVORS of curry, fennel, onion, and olives, this delicious orzo dish is a different way to spice up a whole roasted chicken. For a fun presentation, stuff the chicken with the finished orzo medley before serving.

SERVES: 3-4

¼ cup Madras curry powder

1 tablespoon minced garlic

¼ cup extra-virgin olive oil, plus additional for tossing

1 tablespoon kosher salt

1 whole chicken (4-5 pounds), preferably kosher or naturally raised

2 bulbs fennel, cut into 1-inch pieces

Kosher salt and freshly ground black pepper

1 large red onion, ¼-inch dice

¼ cup chopped pitted black olives

¼ cup chopped pitted green olives

½ cup chopped canned tomatoes (preferably San Marzano)

Juice and minced zest of 1 lemon

1 cup cooked orzo

1 In small bowl, combine curry powder, garlic, ¼ cup olive oil, and salt. Pat chicken dry, then rub inside and out with curry mixture. Let marinate in refrigerator for at least 1 hour or overnight.

2 Preheat oven and copper pan to 500°F. In bowl, combine fennel, olive oil to coat, and salt and pepper and toss to combine. Place fennel and onions in bottom of copper pan in even layer and rest chicken on top of fennel. Bake chicken until browned all over, 15-20 minutes, then lightly cover with foil and turn oven down to 275°F to finish roasting, about 70 minutes total.

3 When chicken is done, let rest on cutting board. Meanwhile, place pan over high heat. Then add olives, tomatoes, lemon juice and zest, and orzo, and season with salt and pepper. If desired, stuff the chicken with the orzo mixture before serving.

Kung Pao Chicken

SERVING CHICKEN AND VEGETABLES CAN GET BORING, so why not dress them up? Draped in a rich Kung Pao sauce and tossed with crunchy peanuts for a little added texture, this chicken is packed with flavor. There's a touch of hot sauce already in the recipe, but feel free to add more if you're big on spice.

SERVES: 2-4

KUNG PAO SAUCE

Grapeseed or canola oil

2 tablespoons minced garlic

2 tablespoons minced ginger

2 tablespoons sambal or Sriracha sauce

½ cup dark soy sauce

1 tablespoon honey

½ cup rice vinegar

1 tablespoon cornstarch mixed with 1 tablespoon water

Kosher salt and freshly ground black pepper

1   In copper pan coated lightly with oil over high heat, add garlic and ginger and sauté for 1 minute, just to soften. Add sambal, and sauté until well-blended.

2   Add soy sauce and scrape bottom of pan, then add honey and vinegar. Bring to a boil and slowly whisk in cornstarch slurry to thicken. Check for flavor and season if necessary. Remove from heat.

CHICKEN

2 large boneless, skinless chicken breasts, cut into ½-inch dice

Kosher salt and freshly ground black pepper

Grapeseed or canola oil

½ cup carrots, ½-inch dice

4 ribs celery, cut into ½-inch dice

1 cup Kung Pao Sauce

½ cup roasted peanuts

Anytime Rice (page 128), for serving

1   In large bowl, season the chicken with salt and pepper. In clean copper pan coated lightly with oil over high heat, add chicken and cook for 2 minutes.

Add carrots, celery, Kung Pao sauce and peanuts and stir-fry for about 1 minute, until combined thoroughly. Serve on a platter over Anytime Rice.

Caramelized Onion–Stuffed Chicken

SOME MEALS ARE SO ELEGANT, you'd think they take all day. Caramelized Onion-Stuffed Chicken is a cinch to make, and all it takes is the help of a toothpick or twine. The soy glaze and caramelized onions are a perfect flavor pair. Serve this with steamed vegetables like bok choy or asparagus.

SERVES: 2-3

2 tablespoons unsalted butter

3 medium red onions, thinly sliced

1 teaspoon kosher salt

¼ teaspoon freshly ground black pepper

2 tablespoons chopped fresh Thai or regular basil

½ cup soy sauce

½ cup rice vinegar

¼ cup packed brown sugar

1 cup grapeseed or canola oil

3 boneless, skinless chicken breast halves, pounded ¼-inch thick

1   Preheat oven to 350°F. In small copper pan or saucepan, melt butter over medium heat. Add onions and stir. Cook, covered, stirring two or three times, until onions are sweet and tender, about 15 minutes. Add salt, pepper, and basil and stir to combine. Remove from heat and set aside.

2   Meanwhile, in large bowl, combine soy sauce, vinegar, and brown sugar and stir until sugar dissolves. Slowly stir in oil.

3   Lay chicken breasts flat and spread one-third of onion mixture onto each piece, leaving a ½-inch border all around. Roll, and poke with a toothpick or tie with kitchen twine to secure. Submerge in marinade and marinate for 1 hour.

4   Shake off excess marinade and transfer chicken to copper pan; bake uncovered until golden, about 30 minutes. Remove toothpick or twine before serving.

Crunchy Peanut Chicken

BREADED CHICKEN IS DELICIOUS, but adding peanuts to the mix makes a crunchy, satisfying version that will appeal to almost everyone. If a peanut allergy is a problem, just swap out the peanuts for sunflower seeds for a similar texture.

SERVES: 2-4

¼ cup unsalted peanuts (can substitute sunflower seeds)

⅓ cup panko (Japanese bread crumbs)

1½ teaspoons kosher salt

½ teaspoon freshly ground black pepper

1 tablespoon olive oil

¼ cup all-purpose flour

2 large eggs, lightly beaten

4 boneless, skinless chicken breast halves

1   Preheat oven to 475°F. Add peanuts to re-sealable plastic bag and use a rolling pin to crush into tiny pieces. Or, pulse in food processor.

2   Add crushed peanuts, panko, salt, and pepper to shallow bowl and mix to combine. Add olive oil and stir until combined. Add flour and eggs to two separate shallow bowls.

3   Dredge chicken in flour until coated on all sides, then dip in egg, then in peanut mixture. Transfer to lightly greased copper pan.

4   Bake uncovered until lightly browned and cooked through, about 15 minutes, flipping once.

Classic Barbecue Pork Ribs

RIBS AREN'T JUST FOR GRILLING. You can make them in the copper pan, too! The key is to let the ribs marinate overnight for the very best flavor. When you cook them in the copper pan, you save yourself the mess of grilling, all while packing in amazing flavor!

SERVES: 2-4

1 tablespoon packed light brown sugar

2 teaspoons garlic powder

2 teaspoons ground cumin

1 teaspoon chili powder

1 teaspoon paprika

⅛ teaspoon cayenne pepper

2 tablespoons kosher salt

1 teaspoon freshly ground black pepper

2 (2-pound) racks baby back ribs, membranes removed

1 cup of your favorite vinegar

½ cup barbecue sauce

1   In small bowl, combine brown sugar, garlic powder, cumin, chili powder, paprika, cayenne, salt, and black pepper. Rub spice mix into ribs, cover, and place in refrigerator for 2 hours or overnight.

2   Preheat oven to 400°F. Place rib racks side-by-side (meaty side up) in the copper pan. Pour the vinegar in so that it covers about ⅛-inch of the pan. Cover with foil and place in the oven to cook for 1½–2 hours.

3   Set oven to broil. Open aluminum foil packet and brush barbecue sauce on ribs. Place under broiler until barbecue sauce turns darker and starts to bubble, 3-5 minutes.

Apple-Onion Pork Chops

LIKE TWO PEAS IN A POD, apples and pork are perfect for each other. The copper pan will brown the meat without sticking, and you can move on to the other steps of the recipe without missing a beat. For best results, brine the pork chops before cooking—it'll help make the pork more tender and succulent. Enjoy this on a cool fall night when apples are in season!

SERVES: 4

⅓ cup kosher salt, for brining, plus more for seasoning

¼ cup sugar, for brining

8 cups water, for brining

1 tablespoon vegetable or olive oil

4 (¾-inch-thick) bone-in pork chops

¼ teaspoon freshly ground black pepper

2 tablespoons unsalted butter

1 medium white onion, sliced

3 semi-tart apples like Braeburn, Cortland, or Honeycrisp, cored and chopped

1 tablespoon 5-spice powder

1 cup apple juice or water

1   If desired, brine pork 2-4 hours in advance: In copper pan, combine salt, sugar, and water. Stir to dissolve salt and sugar and add pork chops. If pork isn't covered, add more water. Refrigerate, covered, for 2-4 hours. Rinse pork and pat dry.

2   In copper pan, heat oil over medium-high heat. Season pork chops with salt and pepper. Add chops to skillet and cook, flipping once, until browned but not cooked through, 3-5 minutes per side. Set aside, covered.

3   In copper pan, melt butter. Add onions and apples and cook, stirring occasionally, until onion slices have started to brown and apples are almost soft, about 8 minutes. Add five spice and apple juice and stir well to combine.

4   Return pork chops to pan and cook until tender, 8-12 minutes, turning halfway through cooking time. Serve with apple-onion mixture on top.

Classic Virginia Ham

CLASSIC VIRGINIA HAM BRINGS EVERYONE TOGETHER. For family holidays or Sunday dinner, this ham recipe is super simple and will have everyone at your table asking for seconds. Serve this ham with all the fixings, and enjoy the special moments as everyone gathers around the table.

SERVES: 8-10

1 (6-8 pound) smoked ham

1 cup packed brown sugar

1 tablespoon balsamic vinegar

½ teaspoon ground mustard

12-15 whole cloves

1   Heat oven to 325°F. Place ham, fat-side up, in copper pan. Tent with foil and bake until ham reaches an internal temperature of 135°F, about 15 minutes per pound.

2   In small bowl, stir together brown sugar, vinegar, and mustard. About 15 minutes before ham is done, remove from oven. Cut diagonal lines in ham in both directions to make a checkerboard pattern and insert cloves into surface of ham where lines intersect. Brush brown sugar mixture onto surface of ham. Bake uncovered until cooked through.

3   Remove ham from copper pan and let stand, covered, about 10 minutes before serving.

Chicken and Mushroom Fricassee

BACON, MUSHROOMS, AND JUICY DRUMSTICKS—what more could you ask for? Using bone-in chicken is always preferable because it won't dry out the way chicken breast frequently does. The best part is, you need only one pan to cook an amazing meal!

SERVES: 4-6

2 pounds bone-in chicken thighs and drumsticks

Kosher salt and freshly ground black pepper

2 tablespoons grapeseed or canola oil

6 slices bacon, cut into ½-inch pieces

1 large white onion, halved and sliced ¼-inch thick

1 tablespoon minced garlic

1 pound button mushrooms, sliced ¼-inch thick

2 tablespoons minced fresh tarragon

2 cups canned whole roma tomatoes, roughly chopped, with juice

1   Preheat oven to 400°F. Season chicken with salt and pepper.

2   Heat copper pan over medium-high heat. Add oil and swirl to coat bottom. When oil is hot, add chicken and cook until brown on both sides, about 10 minutes. Transfer to a plate and set aside. Add the bacon to the pan and cook until browned. Remove the cooked bacon and set aside for later.

3   Drain pan of all but 1 tablespoon fat. Add onion, garlic, and mushrooms and sauté until light brown, 2-3 minutes; season with salt and pepper. Add tarragon, tomatoes with their liquid. Mix well and season with salt and pepper to taste. Top with chicken, transfer to oven, and bake until chicken is cooked through, 20-25 minutes. Transfer to a platter, add the bacon for garnish and serve.

Coq au Vin

A CLASSIC COMFORT FOOD, this French chicken-and-wine concoction is perfect for a cold winter evening. The red wine glaze, bacon, mushrooms, and moist chicken make for a hearty and satisfying meal. Serve it with a nice glass of wine and a fresh baguette for soaking up the rich sauce.

SERVES: 3-4

2 tablespoons canola oil, divided

1 whole chicken (3-4 pounds), cut into 8 pieces

4 slices bacon, chopped

1 cup pearl onions, roughly chopped

1 cup chopped carrots

4 cloves garlic, minced

2 tablespoons minced ginger

1 bunch scallions, green and white parts, cut into 1-inch lengths

2 cups shiitake mushrooms, stemmed and quartered

1 fennel bulb, sliced

1 jalapeño, sliced

Kosher salt and freshly ground black pepper

1 bottle red wine

2 tablespoons soy sauce

4 stalks celery, sliced

1   Preheat oven to 350°F. Heat 1 tablespoon oil in copper pan over medium-high heat. Add chicken in batches and cook until skin is golden brown. Transfer to plate and set aside. Add bacon to the pan and cook until browned. Once nice and brown, remove from pan but keep the bacon fat.

2   Add remaining tablespoon oil, onions, carrots, garlic, ginger, scallions, mushrooms, fennel, and jalapeño. Season with salt and pepper. Sweat vegetables, stirring, for 2-3 minutes, or until vegetables have softened.

3   Add chicken back to pan and stir to combine. Add red wine, soy sauce, and celery. Cover and cook in oven for 75-90 minutes, or until chicken is cooked through. Transfer chicken pieces and vegetables to a large wide bowl and pour sauce over top.

Chili Pork Chops with Brussels Sprouts and Potatoes

A ONE-POT MEAL THAT COVERS ALL THE BASES, these pork chops have a little bit of spice and are cooked with healthy Brussels sprouts and hearty potatoes. The pork chops will brown to perfection and retain all of the flavorful goodness of the spices.

SERVES: 2

⅓ cup kosher salt, for brining, plus more for seasoning

¼ cup sugar, for brining

8 cups water, for brining

2 (8-ounce) pork loin chops

3 tablespoons ancho chili powder, or other chili powder

2 tablespoons packed dark brown sugar

4 tablespoons minced garlic, divided

¼ cup (½ stick) melted unsalted butter

Freshly ground black pepper

3 tablespoons grapeseed or canola oil, divided

2 pints Brussels sprouts, halved and ends trimmed

5 new potatoes, halved

2 tablespoons ponzu or lime juice (optional)

1   If desired, brine pork 2-4 hours in advance: In copper pan, combine salt, sugar, and water. Stir to dissolve salt and sugar and add pork chops. If pork isn't covered, add more water. Refrigerate, covered, for 2-4 hours or overnight. Rinse pork and pat dry.

2   Preheat oven to 350°F. On large shallow plate combine chili powder, brown sugar, 2 tablespoons garlic, and butter and blend. Roll pork in mixture and season lightly with salt and pepper.

3 Heat copper pan over medium heat.
Add 2 tablespoons oil and swirl to coat
pan. When oil is hot, add pork chops
and sauté, turning once, until brown,
about 6 minutes. Transfer chops to plate
and set aside.

pepper and mix well. Top with pork
chops and roast in oven until pork
is medium and registers 140°F on
an instant-read thermometer, 15–20
minutes. Remove and allow to rest
10 minutes.

4 Add remaining tablespoon oil, swirl,
and add Brussels sprouts, potatoes,
remaining 2 tablespoons garlic, and
ponzu, if using. Season with salt and

5 Transfer sprouts and potatoes to
two individual plates, top with pork
chops, and serve.

Thai Curry Pork and Sweet Potatoes

NOT EVERY CURRY IS THE SAME, and that's because curry is a blend of spices that can change depending on preference, culture, or family recipes. With a red curry blend, coconut milk, and some heat from the jalapeños, this pork dish is exceptional. If you prefer other meat, such as chicken, feel free to swap it out.

SERVES: 3-4

1½-2 pounds pork shoulder, trimmed and cut into 1-inch cubes

Kosher salt and freshly ground black pepper

3 tablespoons canola oil, plus more if needed, divided

2 large onions, cut into 1-inch pieces

1 tablespoon minced ginger

2 red jalapeño peppers, minced

1 tablespoon chili powder

1 tablespoon ground coriander

1 tablespoon paprika

1 pound carrots, chopped

2 large sweet potatoes, peeled and cut into 1-inch dice

1 cup unsweetened coconut milk

1 bay leaf

Juice of 1 lime

1 cup rice, cooked for serving

1   Season pork with salt and pepper. Heat copper pan over medium-high heat. Add 2 tablespoons oil and swirl to coat bottom of pan. When oil is hot, and working in batches, add pork, with additional oil if necessary, and brown on all sides, 4-6 minutes. Transfer to a plate and keep warm.

2   To copper pan, add remaining 1 tablespoon oil and swirl to coat. Add onions, ginger, and jalapeños and sauté over medium-high heat, stirring until onions have softened, about 1 minute.

3 Add chili powder, coriander, and paprika, and sauté, stirring, for 30 seconds. Add carrots, sweet potatoes, coconut milk, bay leaf, and enough water to cover vegetables by 1 inch. Adjust seasoning, if necessary, and return pork to pan. If pork isn't completely covered, add more water.

4 Bring to a simmer, cover, and cook until the pork is tender, about 1½ hours. Remove bay leaf and stir in lime juice. Serve with rice.

Sausage & Rice Stuffed Bell Peppers

SUMMER BARBECUES ARE INFINITELY BETTER when you have super fresh, brightly colored vegetables on your plate. Select a rainbow of peppers for this recipe, and choose your favorite kind of sausage. This recipe calls for spicy Italian sausage, but you can even switch it up for sweet chicken sausage or ground beef. Wheat-free tamari sauce makes this completely gluten-free.

SERVES: 4

4 large red, orange, and/or yellow bell peppers

¼ cup + 1 tablespoon canola oil, plus more for coating peppers

Kosher salt and freshly ground black pepper

4 large eggs, beaten

1 pound spicy Italian sausages, casings removed

2 bunches scallions

1 tablespoon minced ginger

1 tablespoon minced garlic

1 jalapeño pepper, minced

4 cups cooked Anytime Rice (page 128)

1 tablespoon wheat-free tamari or soy sauce

½ cup shredded cheddar cheese

1 tablespoon freshly chopped parsley, for garnish

1   Preheat oven to 350°F. Remove stems from bell peppers and cut off tops. Mince tops and set aside.

2   Remove pepper seeds and ribs, coat peppers inside and out in oil, season with salt and pepper, and transfer to square pan. Bake until peppers have softened, 10–12 minutes. Remove from pan and set aside.

3   Season eggs with salt and pepper. Heat pan over high heat. Add ¼ cup oil to the pan and swirl to coat. When oil is almost smoking, add eggs and scramble, stirring constantly, about 15 seconds. Transfer eggs to paper towel–lined plate to drain.

4   Reduce heat to medium-high. Add sausage meat to pan, breaking up with a spoon, until sausage is browned, 6–8 minutes. Transfer to plate and set aside.

5   Thinly chop scallions and reserve 3 tablespoons for garnish.

6   Add remaining 1 tablespoon oil and swirl to coat pan. When oil is hot, add non-reserved scallions, ginger, garlic, and jalapeños. Cook, stirring occasionally, until cooked through, about 3 minutes. Add rice, tamari, eggs, and sausage meat.

7   Stuff peppers with rice mixture. Top with cheese and put back in oven until rice mixture is warmed through and cheese is melted, 5–10 minutes. Garnish with reserved scallions and parsley.

BBQ Pulled Pork

ONE SANDWICH THAT IS WORTH THE WAIT, BBQ Pulled Pork is downright heavenly. A simple mix of spices, a slow-roasted pork shoulder, and some time in the oven makes the pork break apart oh-so-easily. Serve this at a backyard barbecue with traditional sides like corn bread and cole slaw, or make it a special treat for any occasion.

SERVES: 8-10

2 tablespoons ground cumin

3 tablespoons garlic powder

2 tablespoons chili powder

1 tablespoon paprika

2 tablespoons kosher salt

1 tablespoon freshly ground black pepper

1 (6-8 pound) bone-in pork shoulder

1 cup barbecue sauce

Hamburger buns, for serving

1   Preheat oven to 450°F. In small bowl, combine cumin, garlic powder, chili powder, paprika, salt, and pepper.

2   Pat pork dry, then rub spice mixture on all exposed meat (not the skin). Place skin-side-up in square pan.

3   Cook for 20 minutes, then reduce heat to 325°F and continue cooking, 1 hour for every pound of meat, 6–8 hours total. An instant-read thermometer should read 185°F when inserted in center of meat, and meat should easily fall away from the bone. Remove pork from oven and let rest 20–30 minutes.

4   When pork is cool enough to handle, remove from bone and pull apart with your fingers. Thoroughly mix when finished, to evenly distribute the various textures of meat.

5   Add pulled pork to clean square pan and stir in barbecue sauce. Cook, covered with foil, until warm and steaming, about 15 minutes. Serve on hamburger buns with your favorite slaw or pickles.

Sriracha–Orange Chicken with Cauliflower

THIS ISN'T YOUR AVERAGE restaurant orange chicken recipe—it's so much more. The combination of Sriracha, mustard, Worcestershire, and orange creates a flavorful sauce to jazz up bone-in chicken legs. The copper pan browns the chicken just right!

SERVES: 3-4

2 tablespoons sambal or Sriracha sauce

1 tablespoon Dijon mustard

2 tablespoons Worcestershire sauce

Zest and juice of 1 orange

2 pounds whole chicken legs

Kosher salt and freshly ground black pepper

2 tablespoons canola or grapeseed oil

1 red onion, cut into ¼-inch-thick slices

1 head cauliflower, florets and stems

3-4 fresh peaches, halved or quartered

1   Preheat oven to 450°F. Make the marinade: In large bowl, combine sambal, mustard, and Worcestershire sauce. Whisk in orange juice and zest. Season chicken on both sides with salt and add to marinade. Let sit for one hour or up to 8 hours.

2   Heat copper pan over high heat. Add oil and swirl to coat pan. Add chicken, skin-side down and cook for 6–7 minutes, or until skin is golden brown. Turn chicken over and cook for 1-2 minutes. Transfer to a plate and set aside.

3   To same pan, add onion, cauliflower, and peaches and toss to combine. Season with salt and freshly ground black pepper.

4   Lay chicken on top of vegetables and place pan in oven. Cook about 15 minutes, or until chicken is cooked through. Serve right in pan.

Honey-Sesame Spare Ribs

TENDER AND TANGY, these Asian-style spare ribs are braised in vinegar and glazed with a winning combination of honey and hand-squeezed orange juice. These ribs are so good you may not want anything else, but you can serve them with rice and steamed vegetables for good measure.

SERVES: 2-4

2 tablespoons chili powder

2 tablespoons kosher salt

1 tablespoon freshly ground black pepper

2 pounds beef spare ribs

2 cups rice vinegar (more or less may be needed)

½ cup honey

Juice and zest of 1 orange

3 tablespoons toasted sesame seeds, for garnish

1   Preheat oven to 375°F. In small bowl, mix together chili powder, salt, and pepper. In copper pan, rub ribs with spice mix. Cover and refrigerate at least 2 hours or overnight.

2   Remove ribs from refrigerator and let come up to room temperature. Add enough vinegar to copper pan so that it covers bottom ¼ inch of pan. Cover and bake until vinegar evaporates, about 2 hours.

3   Meanwhile, mix honey and orange juice and zest together. Glaze ribs, broil to brown and serve garnished with toasted sesame seeds.

Rosemary Pork Roulade

PERFECT FOR A SPECIAL OCCASION or when you want to wow your guests, Rosemary Pork Roulade is as elegant as it is delicious. If you want to go one step further, top each serving with a spoonful of sautéed apples and onions.

SERVES: 4-6

½ cup grapeseed or canola oil

3 tablespoons minced garlic

¼ cup chopped fresh parsley

¼ cup chopped fresh sage

3 tablespoons chopped fresh rosemary

2 tablespoons ground fennel seed

2 tablespoons orange zest

1 (4-pound) pork loin

¼ cup kosher salt, divided

2 tablespoons freshly ground black pepper

1   Preheat oven to 350°F. In small bowl, combine oil, garlic, parsley, sage, rosemary, fennel, and zest. Set aside.

2   Butterfly pork loin so that it unfolds into a flat slab by making several deep horizontal scores on each side—slicing it so that your knife doesn't cut all the way through the meat. Pound with meat mallet if necessary to get loin thin enough to wrap around filling.

3   Sprinkle half of salt and the pepper on pork, then spread the herb mixture over it, leaving a 1-inch border on all sides. Then roll up loin and secure with butcher's twine. Sprinkle with remaining salt on outside.

4   Place in copper pan, cover, and cook until pork reaches internal temperature of 145°F, about 2½ hours. Baste several times during cooking, if desired. During last 15 minutes of cooking time, uncover so that pork browns. Remove twine and let rest for 10-15 minutes before carving.

Bacon-Wrapped Sirloin

THIS RECIPE NEEDS NO INTRODUCTION. Steak plus bacon means dinner is served. If you absolutely require something else on your plate, you can serve this with just about any veggie, and tastes great with roasted potatoes.

SERVES: 4

4 sirloin steaks, around 1½-inches thick

Kosher salt and freshly ground black pepper

4 slices bacon

1 tablespoon unsalted butter

2 tablespoons grapeseed or canola oil

1   Preheat oven to 450°F. Generously season both sides of steak with salt and pepper. Wrap each steak with 1 slice bacon and secure with toothpick.

2   Heat copper pan over medium-high heat. Add butter and oil. When melted, add steak to pan and cook until browned, about 1 minute per side.

3   Place copper pan in oven and cook, covered, until desired doneness is reached, 7–10 minutes for medium-rare.

4   Remove from oven and allow to rest for 5 minutes before serving.

Steak with Dijon–Mushroom Sauce

THIS ROBUST DISH IS PERFECT FOR RED MEAT LOVERS EVERYWHERE. Better than grilling, the copper pan lets you sear the steaks just right and cook up the mushroom sauce all in one spot. The thick, tangy sauce and hearty mushrooms are a perfect complement to the tenderloin. Serve with sautéed vegetables or mashed potatoes for a well-rounded meal.

SERVES: 4

4 (6-ounce) center-cut beef tenderloin steaks

Kosher salt and freshly ground black pepper

2 tablespoons extra-virgin olive oil, divided

4 ounces mushrooms, such as shiitake or cremini, sliced

1 large red onion, finely chopped

2 teaspoons all-purpose flour

¼ cup beef broth

¼ cup dry white wine

1 tablespoon Dijon mustard

1   Preheat oven to 450°F. Rub steaks with salt and pepper.

2   Heat copper pan over medium-high heat and add 1 tablespoon oil. Sear steaks over medium high heat until browned, about 3 minutes per side. Set the steaks aside.

3   Add the remaining 1 tablespoon of oil and sauté the onions and mushrooms until slightly tender. Add the steak on top of the onions and mushrooms. Transfer the skillet to the oven and cook the steaks until an instant-read thermometer inserted in the thickest part registers 125°F, 6–8 minutes. Transfer steaks to a plate and let rest, covered with foil for 5 minutes.

4   While steak is resting, sprinkle the vegetables with flour and stir to coat, 30–60 seconds. Add broth and wine and cook, stirring frequently, until thick enough to coat the back of a spoon, 2–4 minutes. Remove from heat. Stir in mustard until well combined and pour over steaks before serving.

Mussels in Chorizo– White Wine Broth

MUSSELS IN WHITE WINE BROTH ARE ALREADY AMAZING, but adding Spanish Chorizo really takes it up a notch. The chorizo offers a spicy counterpoint to the mussels, and adds incredible flavor to the broth. Serve with crostini or a crusty baguette for dipping.

SERVES: 4

2 tablespoons olive oil

3 ounces dried Spanish chorizo, casing removed and thinly sliced

2 cloves garlic, crushed

1 teaspoon ground fennel seeds

1 pint cherry or grape tomatoes, halved

¼ cup dry white wine

Kosher salt and freshly ground black pepper

4 pounds mussels, scrubbed and de-bearded

2 tablespoons butter

1 tablespoon chopped fresh parsley

4 slices crusty bread, for serving

1   Heat oil in copper pan over medium heat. Add chorizo and cook, stirring occasionally, until chorizo begins to brown and crisp, about 4 minutes. Add garlic and fennel seeds and cook, stirring, until fragrant, about 1 minute. Add tomatoes and mussels, season with salt and pepper. Cook until reduced by three-quarters, 5–8 minutes.

2   Add wine, cover and cook, stirring occasionally, until mussels open, 6–8 minutes. Discard any mussels that did not open. Remove mussels to a bowl and add butter to the pan. Reduce the liquid by one third and pour over the mussels. Sprinkle with parsley and serve with crusty bread.

Pancetta Mashed Potatoes

PANCETTA, LEEKS, AND BUTTER make these mashed potatoes out of this world. If you don't have pancetta, you can use thick-cut bacon, and they will be just as delicious. If you're a mashed potato aficionado, these are for you.

SERVES: 4-6

4 medium Yukon gold potatoes, peeled and chopped

2 ounces pancetta or 3 thick slices bacon, cut into small chunks

2 teaspoons canola oil

2 cups chopped leeks, white and pale green parts only

2 tablespoons unsalted butter

⅓ cup whole milk or half-and-half

Kosher salt and freshly ground black pepper

2 tablespoons chopped scallions, for garnish (optional)

1   Fill copper pan three-quarters full with water and potatoes. Heat over high heat and boil potatoes until tender, 15-20 minutes. Drain and set potatoes aside.

2   Over medium heat, cook the pancetta or bacon until browned, about 10 minutes. Drain all but 1 teaspoon fat from copper pan. Reduce heat to medium-low. Add oil and leeks; sauté until leeks are tender, about 6-8 minutes.

3   Remove pan from heat. Add potatoes back to pan with butter and milk and mash with potato masher until fluffy. Stir in pancetta or bacon and season with salt and pepper to taste. Garnish with scallions, if desired.

Salmon with Tomato Tapenade

THIS OLIVE OIL-POACHED SALMON RECIPE IS A STUNNER. Draped in the flavors of olive and tomato tapenade and a dose of lemon, the salmon absolutely shines. Make sure to use extra-virgin olive oil and not regular olive oil—it makes a difference!

SERVES: 4

1 cup extra-virgin olive oil

1 tablespoon fermented black beans (optional)

1 cup pitted niçoise olives or other oil-cured black olives

1 large onion, thinly sliced

2 pints fresh cherry tomatoes, or 1 (28-ounce) can plum tomatoes, drained, crushed to remove as much juice as possible, and coarsely chopped

Kosher salt and freshly ground black pepper

4 (6- to 8-ounce) salmon fillets, skinned

Leaves from 1 bunch Thai or regular basil

3 cups watercress

2 lemons, one juiced and zested, the other cut into wedges

1   Preheat oven to 250°F. Heat oil in copper pan over medium heat until hot. Add black beans, if using, olives, and onion and cook until onion is soft and mixture is simmering, 3–5 minutes. Add tomatoes, season with salt and pepper, and simmer until tomatoes have softened, about 8 minutes.

2   Transfer three-quarters of mixture to medium bowl. Season salmon with salt and pepper. Add salmon to pan skin-side up and top with handful of basil. Spoon remaining tapenade over salmon so that fish is completely submerged. Cover with lid and bake for 6–8 minutes for medium.

3   Place a handful of watercress on individual plates, drizzle with lemon juice, and season with salt and pepper. Using a slotted spoon, transfer salmon to plates atop the watercress, top with tapenade, garnish with lemon zest, and serve with lemon wedge.

Braised Red Wine Pot Roast

THE COPPER PAN ISN'T JUST FOR SAUTÉING OR ROASTING—it can braise, too! Placing the lid on the copper pan will capture all of the delicious juice from the roast, making it perfectly tender. The best part is, you can use the braising liquid as a gravy to pour over the roughly mashed potatoes.

SERVES: 4-6

4 medium Yukon gold potatoes, quartered

1 (4-5 pound) pot roast

Kosher salt and freshly ground black pepper

Canola or grapeseed oil

1 tablespoon minced garlic

2 teaspoons minced ginger

1 tablespoon minced fermented black beans (optional)

4 scallions, sliced thinly

2 cups dry red wine

2 tablespoons soy sauce

2 cups chopped carrots

1 sprig rosemary

1   Preheat oven to 250°F. Wrap potatoes in foil and pierce several times with fork. Set aside.

2   Season beef generously with salt and pepper. Heat copper pan over medium-high heat. Add oil and swirl to coat bottom. When oil is hot, add beef and cook on all sides until brown, about 15 minutes. Transfer to a plate and set aside.

3   Pour off all but 2 tablespoons of the fat from pan. Add garlic, ginger, black beans, if using, and scallions and cook, stirring frequently, until softened, about 2 minutes. Stir in red wine, soy sauce, carrots, and rosemary, and season with salt and pepper. Add the meat back to the pan, cover, and transfer to the oven. Cook until a fork easily pierces meat, about 4 hours. After 2½ hours of cooking, place potatoes in oven.

4 Remove pan and potatoes and allow meat to stand in its liquid, covered, for 20 minutes, then transfer roast to a carving board and allow to rest for 5 more minutes. Meanwhile, on stovetop, heat copper pan with braising liquid over high heat until reduced slightly, about 5 minutes.

5 Slice half the roast into ⅛-inch-thick slices and transfer slices plus remaining half roast to pan. Spoon potatoes into medium bowl and mash roughly. Bring pan and potatoes to table, and serve with reduced braising liquid.

Asian-Style Sloppy Joes

NOT YOUR AVERAGE SLOPPY JOES, this recipe calls for an Asian twist to the classic American meal. Sautéed with ingredients like ginger, hot sauce, and hoisin sauce, the meat will be kicking with flavor. You can find hoisin sauce in the international foods aisle at the grocery store.

SERVES: 6

2 tablespoons grapeseed or canola oil

2 medium onions, cut into ¼-inch dice

2 tablespoons minced garlic

1 tablespoon minced ginger

1 cup diced celery

2 tablespoons sambal or hot sauce of your choice

1¼ cups hoisin sauce

1 pound ground beef

1 pound ground pork

Juice of 2 limes

2 cups diced roma tomatoes, canned

Kosher salt and freshly ground black pepper

6 hamburger buns, toasted

1 small head iceberg lettuce, shredded

Chips and pickles, for serving

1   Heat copper pan over high heat. Add oil and swirl to coat bottom. When oil is hot, add onions, garlic, ginger, celery, and sambal. Sauté, stirring occasionally, until onions are soft, about 2 minutes. Add hoisin sauce and sauté 1 minute. Add beef and pork and sauté, breaking up meat, until just cooked through, about 6 minutes. Add lime juice and tomatoes and season with salt and pepper. Reduce heat to medium-low and simmer until the mixture has thickened enough to form mounds when ladled, 20-25 minutes. Taste for seasoning and adjust with salt and pepper to taste if needed.

2   Top bun bottoms generously with meat mixture. Top with lettuce and bun tops. Serve with chips and pickles.

Mustard-Crusted Salmon with Asparagus

YOU WOULDN'T THINK OF PUTTING MUSTARD on many kinds of fish, but with salmon, it's a game-changer. The spicy Dijon is a great balance to tender salmon, and the copper pot cooks everything evenly. Baked asparagus is an easy-to-prepare, healthy addition to your plate.

SERVES: 2

1 bunch asparagus (about 1 pound)

2 tablespoons olive oil

Kosher salt and freshly ground black pepper

2 (6-ounce) skin-on salmon fillets

1½ tablespoons whole-grain Dijon mustard

⅛ teaspoon paprika

2 tablespoons chopped fresh tarragon

1   Preheat oven to 275°F. In large bowl, toss asparagus with oil, salt, and pepper. Lay asparagus in single layer on parchment paper–lined square pan, and bake for 5 minutes. Remove asparagus to plate.

2   Spread mustard over tops of salmon fillets. Season with additional salt and pepper and paprika.

3   Heat copper pan over medium-high heat. Add salmon fillets, skin side up. Cook, turning once, until salmon is firm and crispy, but still pink in center, about 8 minutes. Sprinkle with tarragon before serving.

Copper Pan Meatloaf

CLASSIC MEATLOAF IS ALWAYS COOKED in a loaf pan, but despite tradition, this doesn't actually result in the best-tasting meatloaf! Form the meat into a loaf shape, but don't make it as big as the copper pan itself. By leaving extra space, you'll get a perfectly browned meatloaf. What's more, you can roast vegetables in the same pan, just like you would if you were roasting a chicken.

SERVES: 4-6

1½ pounds total ground meat (⅓ pork and the rest can be beef, veal or dark chicken meat)

1 cup Italian-seasoned bread crumbs or cooked rice

1 medium yellow onion, grated

1 tablespoon Worcestershire sauce

1 tablespoon soy sauce

1 teaspoon garlic powder

1 large egg, beaten

1 teaspoon kosher salt

1 tablespoon freshly ground black pepper

½ cup ketchup

2 tablespoons light brown sugar

1 Preheat oven to 375°F. In medium bowl, loosely mix together all ingredients except ketchup and brown sugar. In small bowl, combine ketchup and brown sugar and mix well.

2 Form meat mixture into loaf. Place in the pan and put a piece of foil on top of the loaf. Press down foil to form it around the loaf.

3 Bake until loaf is cooked through and instant-read thermometer inserted into center reaches 160°F, about 80 minutes. About 15-20 minutes before meatloaf is done, remove top layer of foil and spread ketchup mixture on top and sides. Let cool 10 minutes before serving.

Baked Cod with Zucchini

WHITE FISH AND ZUCCHINI ARE A GREAT MATCH for a healthy, simple dinner. Wrap everything in foil packets, pop them in the copper pan, and soon you'll have a perfectly steamed meal. For added color, use both green and yellow zucchini!

SERVES: 4

4 (6-ounce) cod fillets or other mild white fish

Kosher salt and freshly ground black pepper

3 zucchini, sliced into thin rounds

2 tablespoons dry white wine

2 tablespoons extra-virgin olive oil

1 lemon, sliced

4 sprigs fresh thyme

1   Preheat oven to 450°F. Season fish with salt and pepper and place each fillet on a piece of foil. Arrange zucchini around each fillet. Drizzle a quarter of the wine and a quarter of the oil into each fish packet.

2   Place several slices of lemon on top of each fillet and top with thyme sprig. Wrap foil around fish and vegetables, leaving some space at top of each packet; close tightly so that steam does not escape. Place packets in copper pan and bake until fish is cooked through, about 8 minutes. Open packets carefully and let sit for a minute or two before serving.

Cacio e Pepe

AN ADULT VERSION OF PASTA WITH BUTTER, Cacio e Pepe is simple but elegant. Coated in fresh grated cheese and ground black pepper, this spaghetti dish is comforting and delicious. If you want to make this extra special, use fresh spaghetti.

SERVES: 3-4

1 (16-ounce) package spaghetti pasta

1–3 tablespoons freshly ground black pepper

6 tablespoons unsalted butter

6 tablespoons extra-virgin olive oil

Kosher salt

½ cup grated Parmigiano-Reggiano cheese

¼ cup grated Pecorino Romano cheese, and some for garnish

1   Bring large pot of salted water to boil over high heat; cook pasta according to package directions. Drain pasta and reserve ½ cup pasta water. Keep warm.

2   Meanwhile, heat copper pan over medium heat, add pepper, and toast, stirring, until fragrant, about 20 seconds.

Place in small bowl and set aside. Add butter and oil to copper pan and cook, stirring occasionally, until butter has melted. Add ¼ cup reserved pasta water and stir to combine. Then add pasta and cheese and stir to coat. If more moisture is needed, add more pasta water. Season with toasted pepper and salt, top with cheese, and serve immediately.

Perfect Mac and Cheese

CREAMY, CHEESY, AND OH-SO-GOOD, you can have this mac and cheese on your plate in no time! The panko crumbs add a little bit of texture to this super delicious meal. Bring this to a pot luck or backyard barbecue to share with friends, or serve it on a cozy night.

SERVES: 6-8

1 (16-ounce) package pasta

2 cups shredded Cheddar cheese

1 quart heavy cream

1 tablespoon cornstarch

1 cup water

¼ cup panko (Japanese bread crumbs) toasted with butter

1   Place all ingredients except panko in copper pan and mix well. Cook, covered, over low heat, until noodles are cooked through and bottom begins to brown, 10-15 minutes.

2   Flip out into a serving bowl to serve. Top with panko.

Roasted Garlic & Cherry Tomatoes

CHERRY TOMATOES, when perfectly ripe in the summer, are so refreshing that you can just snack on them as is. For a fresh addition to meal time that's bursting with flavor, serve these garlicky tomatoes with just about anything. If you're just looking for a quick bite, spoon this mixture onto crostini or toast for a bruschetta-like snack.

SERVES: 3-4

2 pints cherry tomatoes, halved

6 cloves garlic, minced

2 tablespoons extra-virgin olive oil

1 teaspoon kosher salt

½ teaspoon freshly ground black pepper

1   Preheat oven to 375°F. In copper pan, toss together tomatoes, garlic, olive oil, salt, and pepper and spread tomatoes into a single layer. Bake until tomatoes are soft, about 20 minutes.

Anytime Rice

JUST LIKE THE NAME SAYS, this rice is perfect any time. Whether you're serving it as a side or mixing it with stir fry, this blend of two styles of rice is no-fuss, and solves the age-old dilemma of choosing between white rice and brown rice.

SERVES: 4-6

1½ cups brown rice

1½ cups long-grain white rice

Water

1   Rinse brown rice and let soak in fresh cold water to cover for about 1 hour. In the meantime, rinse the white rice by filling a bowl with water and stirring by hand. Drain and repeat until the water in the bowl is clear.

2   Add both the brown and the white rice to a saucepan. Flatten the rice with your palm. With your palm still resting on the rice, add water until it touches the highest knuckle of your middle finger. Cover and boil over high heat for 15 minutes. Reduce the heat to medium and simmer for 20 minutes. Turn off the heat and let the rice stand, covered, to plump, 10 minutes. Stir gently and serve.

New England Shellfish Boil

YOU DON'T NEED TO BE SEASIDE to have an incredible seafood dinner. With the copper pan, you can put together any or all of these shellfish favorites, cook them up in a nice white wine broth, and savor it all with a glass of wine or bread for dipping.

SERVES: 4-6

½ cup (1 stick) butter

3 large onions, chopped

4 ribs celery, chopped

5 cloves garlic, minced

1 bay leaf

Kosher salt and freshly ground black pepper

1 cup chicken stock

2 cups dry white wine

4 pounds mixed shellfish, such as shrimp, clams, mussels, lobster tails, and crab

3 tablespoons chopped fresh parsley

1 lemon, cut into wedges, for serving

1   In copper pan, melt butter. Add onions, celery, and garlic. Cook until onions are translucent and celery begins to soften, about 3-5 minutes. Season with salt and pepper. Add chicken stock and white wine, and bring to a simmer. Add clams and mussels and cook for 5 minutes. Next add the lobster, crab and shrimp and cook for an additional 8-10 minutes.

2   Remove all ingredients from pan and arrange on platter. Pour some of cooking liquid on top, if desired. Sprinkle with parsley and serve with lemon wedges for spritzing.

Scalloped Potatoes

CHEESY, CREAMY, AND COMFORTING, Scalloped Potatoes are the mac and cheese of the potato world. Serve these at a big family dinner with roasted ham or a whole roasted chicken. They'll be a hit!

SERVES: 4-6

3 tablespoons unsalted butter

1 medium yellow onion, finely chopped

2 cloves garlic, minced

3 tablespoons all-purpose flour

½ teaspoon kosher salt

¼ teaspoon freshly ground black pepper

2½ cups 2% milk, warmed

1½ cups shredded Cheddar cheese, divided

5 medium white potatoes, peeled and thinly sliced

1   Preheat oven to 350°F. In small saucepan, melt butter over medium heat. Add onion and cook until almost tender, about 3 minutes. Add garlic and cook 1 minute more.

2   To same saucepan, add flour, salt, and pepper and stir constantly until thickened, about 1 minute. Slowly add milk, stirring constantly, until thickened, about 3 minutes.

3   Reduce heat to low. Add ¼ cup Cheddar cheese. When melted (20-30 seconds), stir to combine. Add remaining Cheddar cheese and repeat.

4   Spread small amount of sauce over bottom of lightly greased square pan. Place half of potatoes, slightly overlapping, on bottom of pan. Cover with half of remaining sauce. Layer remaining potatoes over sauce and top with remaining sauce.

5   Bake, covered, for 45 minutes. Then uncover and bake until potatoes are tender and cheese is bubbly and just starting to brown, 20-25 minutes more. Let sit for 5 minutes before serving.

Delicious Desserts

Peanut Butter Chocolate Chip Cookies

WHEN TWO OF THE BEST KINDS OF COOKIES come together, you can't go wrong. Smooth peanut butter cookies team up with chocolate chips to make a batch you just cannot resist. This batch can serve a whole crowd, but you'll be tempted to keep it all to yourself.

SERVES: 8-10

½ cup smooth peanut butter

½ cup (1 stick) unsalted butter, softened

1 cup packed brown sugar

½ cup granulated sugar

2 large eggs

2 tablespoons light corn syrup

2 tablespoons water

2 teaspoons vanilla extract

2½ cups all-purpose flour

1 teaspoon baking soda

½ teaspoon kosher salt

2 cups semisweet chocolate chips

1   Preheat oven to 375° F. In large bowl, cream together peanut butter, butter, brown sugar, and granulated sugar until smooth. Beat in eggs one at a time, then stir in corn syrup, water, and vanilla. In separate bowl, combine flour, baking soda, and salt; stir into peanut butter mixture. Fold in chocolate chips.

2   Working in batches, spoon cookie dough 3 inches apart onto ungreased copper pan. Bake until edges are golden, 12-14 minutes.

3   Allow cookies to cool for 1 minute in copper pan before removing to cooling racks to cool completely. Repeat with remaining dough.

Chocolate Whoopie Pies

A MASH-UP MADE IN HEAVEN, Whoopie Pies are a cross between cake and cookies. A New England favorite since the early 20th century, the whoopie pie is the official "state treat" of Maine. Traditionally, this incredible dessert is chocolate cake sandwiches with buttercream or other types of frosting. Whoopie pies have since evolved into all sorts of cake flavors, from red velvet to gingerbread.

SERVES: 4-6

3 cups sugar

1 cup (2 sticks) unsalted butter, softened

4 large eggs

½ cup vegetable oil

2 teaspoons vanilla extract

6 cups all-purpose flour

2 cups unsweetened cocoa powder

1½ tablespoons baking soda

1 teaspoon baking powder

1 teaspoon kosher salt

3 cups 2% milk

1 (12-ounce) container whipped-style frosting

1   Preheat oven to 350°F. In a large bowl, beat sugar, butter, and eggs together with electric mixer on medium until well combined, about 3 minutes. Add oil and vanilla and beat again for 1 minute.

2   In separate large bowl, combine all dry ingredients. Add half of dry mixture to sugar mixture and beat until blended. Add half of milk, then remaining dry mixture, then remaining milk, fully incorporating each addition.

3   Working in batches, with ice cream scoop or large serving spoon, scoop circles of batter onto lightly greased copper pan. Bake for 10-12 minutes or until toothpick inserted in center comes out clean. Let cool in copper pan for 1 minute before removing to cooling rack; repeat with remaining batter.

4   When all circles have cooled, spread frosting onto flat side of half of circles and place remaining circles on top to form whoopie pies.

Deep-Fried Sandwich Cookies

NO NEED TO HEAD OUT TO A COUNTY FAIR to get your deep-fried fix. Use your copper pan to deep fry these cookies in pancake mix. The result will make you want to fry every dessert you can get your hands on!

SERVES: 8-10

Vegetable oil, for frying

1 large egg

1 cup milk

2 teaspoons vegetable or canola oil

1 cup dry pancake mix

1 (18-ounce) package sandwich cookies

Powdered sugar, for sprinkling

1 Fill copper pan ⅓ way with oil, add fryer basket if available, and heat over high until oil reaches 375°F.

2 In medium bowl, whisk together egg, milk, and 2 teaspoons oil until smooth Stir in pancake mix until just smooth.

3 Working in batches, dip cookies into batter and then place in copper pan. Fry until golden brown, about 2 minutes. Drain on paper towels and repeat with remaining cookies. Sprinkle with powdered sugar.

Cherry Red Velvet Layer Cake

THERE'S SOMETHING ENCHANTING about red velvet cake, and adding layers of cherry pie filling and frosting makes it even more lovely. Vanilla frosting is probably best for this cake, but you can try chocolate or another flavor of your choice.

SERVES: 6-8

1 cup (2 sticks) unsalted butter, softened

3 cups sugar

4 large eggs

1 tablespoon vanilla extract

¼ cup unsweetened cocoa powder, plus extra for dusting

1 teaspoon red gel food coloring

2 teaspoons kosher salt

2 teaspoons baking soda

4 cups all-purpose flour, sifted

2 cups buttermilk

2 tablespoons white vinegar

2 (12- or 14-ounce) containers whipped-style frosting

1 (21-ounce) can cherry pie filling

1   Heat oven to 350°F. In large bowl, beat butter and sugar together with electric mixer. Add eggs one at a time and beat vigorously until each is incorporated. Mix in vanilla.

2   In separate bowl, add cocoa powder and food coloring. Add approximately 1 teaspoon of water and mix well, adding more water as necessary, until a paste forms. Blend into butter mixture.

3   Sift together salt, baking soda, and flour in a separate bowl. Alternating in 2 batches each, add dry ingredients and buttermilk to butter mixture. In the last batch of buttermilk, mix the vinegar in with the milk before adding to the batter. Mix until blended.

4   Lightly grease copper pan and dust with cocoa powder. Pour one-third of batter into pan and bake until cake springs back lightly when touched, 20–25 minutes. Let cake cool for 5 minutes before flipping onto cooling rack. Repeat with remaining batter until you have three baked and cooled cake layers.

5   To assemble, place one cake layer flat-side down on a serving platter. Spread frosting evenly over top, then top with a layer of cherry pie filling. Place second layer flat-side down on top of first layer, and top with frosting and cherry pie filling. Repeat with remaining layer, frosting, and pie filling.

Double Chocolate Cookies

CHOCOLATE LOVERS, UNITE! Chocolate batter and chocolate chips make these cookies extra decadent. If you want to get the most out of the chocolatey goodness packed in every bite, sprinkle a little hint of salt on the cookies before eating.

SERVES: 8-10

½ cup (1 stick) unsalted butter, softened

1½ cups packed brown sugar

2 large eggs

1 teaspoon vanilla extract

½ cup unsweetened cocoa powder

1 teaspoon baking soda

1 teaspoon kosher salt

2 cups all-purpose flour

1 cup dark chocolate chips

1   Preheat oven to 375° F. Beat butter and sugar with electric mixer until mixture is fluffy, about 3 minutes.

2   Mix in eggs one at a time until incorporated. Add in vanilla, cocoa powder, baking soda, and salt. Mix until everything is incorporated. Stir in flour and chocolate chunks. Mix until just combined.

3   Line copper pan with parchment paper. Working in batches, drop rounded tablespoons of dough 2 inches apart.

4   Bake until edges darken, 10-12 minutes. Allow cookies to cool in copper pan for 1 minute before transferring to cooling rack. Repeat with remaining dough.

Giant Apple Pie

THIS IS THE MOTHER OF ALL APPLE PIES. Use the square copper pan for four times the fun with this huge apple pie. Perfect for serving a large crowd on the holidays (especially Thanksgiving!), there will be plenty of this apple pie for everyone! Scoop vanilla ice cream or whipped cream on each slice when serving.

SERVES: 8-10

4 refrigerated pie crusts

4 (20-ounce) cans apple pie filling

1 tablespoon five spice

All-purpose flour, for dusting

2 egg whites lightly beaten with 2 teaspoons water, for brushing

Vanilla ice cream, for serving

1   Preheat oven to 350°F. Drape 2 pie crusts over bottom and sides of copper pan. In a large bowl mix together the apple pie filling with the five spice. Pour apple pie filling into pie crust.

2   Place remaining pie crusts with edges overlapping on dusted surface and press together to form one sheet. Place over apple filling and pierce in several places with a fork. Brush top of pie with egg wash.

3   Place pan in oven and bake for 45–60 minutes, until pie is golden brown. Let cool slightly before cutting and topping each slice with a scoop of ice cream to serve.

Crunchy Caramel Popcorn

SNACK ON THIS! Whether you have a hankering for sweet and salty caramel popcorn to munch on, or you want to try something new as a light dessert, this easy recipe will do the trick. The sound of popcorn popping right from your copper pan is enough to get you excited about this tasty treat!

SERVES: 2-4

⅓ cup popcorn kernels

Kosher salt

1 cup packed
brown sugar

½ cup half-and-half

¼ cup (½ stick)
unsalted butter

½ teaspoon kosher salt

1 tablespoon
vanilla extract

1 Heat copper pan, covered, over medium-high heat for 2–3 minutes. When hot, add popcorn kernels, cover, and shake. Once kernels start popping, shake copper pan every 10 seconds to mix the kernels. When kernels stop popping, in 2–5 minutes, remove from heat. Pour popcorn into bowl, salt to taste, and set aside.

2 Reduce heat to medium-low. In copper pan, mix brown sugar, half-and-half, butter, and salt. Cook while whisking gently for 5–7 minutes, until sauce thickens. Add vanilla and cook another minute to thicken further. Remove from heat, cool slightly, and pour sauce over popcorn. Toss well to coat.

Deep-Fried Raspberry Cheesecake Balls

THIS DESSERT MAKES CAKE POPS LOOK AMATEUR. Wow your family, friends, or just yourself by making indulgent deep-fried cheesecake balls, with homemade raspberry sauce to go with it. You'll never want to go back to regular cheesecake!

SERVES: 10-12

CHEESECAKE BALLS

1 (17-ounce) frozen cheesecake

1¼ cups all-purpose flour

1 teaspoon baking powder

¼ teaspoon kosher salt

¼ cup sugar

1 cup plus 2 tablespoons milk

2 teaspoons canola oil, plus additional for frying

1   Cut cheesecake into 1-inch cubes and place back in freezer until ready to use.

2   In large bowl, whisk together flour, baking powder, salt, and sugar. Add milk and oil, and whisk until the batter is mostly smooth.

3   Fill copper pan half full of oil, add fryer basket if available, and heat over medium-high until oil reaches 360°F.

4   Working in batches, roll cheesecake cubes in your hands until they become slightly rounded, then immerse in batter and add to square pan. Fry until golden brown, turning if necessary, until browned, 2–3 minutes. Repeat with remaining cheesecake. Let cool for several minutes before serving.

RASPBERRY SAUCE

1 cup frozen raspberries   3-4 tablespoons sugar

1   Warm frozen raspberries in saucepan over the stove until they start to break down. Pour into blender or food processor and blend until smooth, straining the purée to remove seeds, if desired. Return to saucepan and add sugar. Cook, stirring occasionally, until sugar is dissolved and sauce is warm, about 5 minutes

S'mores Cake

WHO NEEDS A CAMPFIRE WHEN YOU HAVE A COPPER PAN? Make this fun s'mores-inspired cake at home, and enjoy the crunchy graham-cracker crust, the chocolatey cake, and the melted marshmallows. You may return to the campfire for the novelty, but you'll stick with this cake for the taste.

SERVES: 6-8

1 (14.4-ounce) box graham crackers

⅓ cup sugar

¼ cup (1½ sticks) unsalted butter, melted

1 (15.25-ounce) box chocolate cake mix

Eggs and oil as called for on box directions

1 (11.5-ounce) bag milk chocolate chips

1 (10-ounce) bag mini marshmallows

1   Preheat oven to 325°F. Break up half the graham crackers and place in bowl of food processor along with half the sugar. Pulse to further break down crackers, then process continuously until crackers are crushed into fine crumbs. Place in a large bowl and repeat with second half of graham crackers and sugar. Alternatively, place crackers in a re-sealable plastic bag and crush with a rolling pin until broken into fine crumbs.

2   Add melted butter to crumbs and stir until crumbs are moist and hold together when clumped. If they don't, add a bit of water.

3   Pour crumbs into copper pan and press evenly into bottom and up sides of pan.

4   In bowl, mix cake according to package directions. Fold in chocolate chips. Pour over crust.

5   Bake, uncovered, until cake is cooked through, 50–60 minutes. Twenty minutes before end of cook time, add mini marshmallows.

Double Chocolate Brownie Sandwich

SOME MIGHT SAY TWO LAYERS OF BROWNIE would be unnecessary in a dessert, and they would be wrong. This mammoth treat layers two different types of brownies—chocolate chip brownies and fudge brownies—to form a brownie sandwich with cream cheese frosting in the center. You're welcome!

SERVES: 10-12

1 (18-ounce) box traditional brownie mix

Vegetable oil and eggs as called for on brownie mix boxes

1 (12-ounce) package chocolate or other chips

1 (18-ounce) box fudge brownie mix

1 (16-ounce) container cream cheese frosting

1 Preheat oven to 325°F. In large bowl, prepare traditional brownies as directed on package, adding chocolate chips to batter before baking.

2 Pour into lightly greased square pan and cook until toothpick inserted in center comes out clean, 25-45 minutes (depending on size of pan).

3 Let cool for 5 minutes, then flip pan over and turn brownie sheet out onto cooling rack (cut brownie sheet first if you're having trouble getting it out of the pan). Clean pan.

4 In large bowl, prepare fudge brownies according to package directions, pour into lightly greased copper pan, and cook until toothpick inserted in center comes out clean, 25-45 minutes (depending on size of pan). Let cool for 10 minutes.

5 When cool, spread frosting evenly over fudge brownies. Then add other brownie sheet on top. Cut into squares to serve.

Index